RELIGIOUS FREEDOM ON TRIAL

O. CARROLL ARNOLD

Judson Press ® Valley Forge

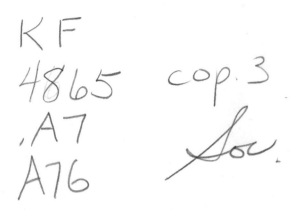

RELIGIOUS FREEDOM ON TRIAL

Unless otherwise indicated, Bible quotations in this volume are in accordance with the Revised Standard Version of the Bible, copyrighted 1952 and 1971 by the Division of Christian Education of the National Council of the Churches of Christ in the United States of America, and are used by permission.

Library of Congress Cataloging in Publication Data

Arnold, Otto Carroll.
  Religious freedom on trial.

  Bibliography: p. 107
  1. Religious liberty—United States—Cases. 2.   United States. Supreme Court. I.
  Title.
KF4865.A7A76   342′.73′085   77-25066
ISBN 0-8170-0778-4

Foreword

The free exercise of religion has become in recent years an issue of growing concern in the nation. Although guaranteed by the First Amendment of the Constitution, it has come under close scrutiny and interpretation only within the past thirty years. Beginning with the *Everson* case in 1947, the United States Supreme Court made this amendment applicable to the several states on the precedent that the Fourteenth Amendment's provision that no liberty is to be denied a citizen without due process is explicitly applicable to the states. Since then, a wide variety of cases have appeared before the Court that have challenged not only religion's privileged position and the particular assumptions of a "Protestant Establishment" in the country but also the doctrine of an absolute separation of church and state.

O. Carroll Arnold, the author, has provided in this book a timely analysis of the factors which have led to this situation. He notes, for example, the political reasons that have caused Americans to view the relations between church and state differently now than they did at the mid-century. He observes that the long-time support of an "absolute separation" between church and state by a Protestant system has been softened since Vatican II and the election of John F. Kennedy, a Roman Catholic, to the presidency in the 1960s. The new "era of good feeling," reflects, he believes, a new recognition and acceptance of pluralism by Protestants, Roman Catholics, and Jews alike fortified by a secular trend of thinking, with its indifference to religious values.

With commendable historical insight, Arnold notes that the First Amendment locks in creative tension two phrases—that Congress shall make no law *respecting an establishment of religion* or *prohibiting the free exercise* thereof—so that one must not dominate the other to the peril of religious liberty. It is his conviction that the founding fathers thus manifested a concern that the free exercise of religion is essential to the morality of society. Indeed, he insists that the voice and influence of the churches should not be withdrawn from public affairs and issues of government.

The perpetuation for 150 years of a Protestant ethic and morality that dominated the public school system and American life generally, albeit without legal sanction, was not seriously challenged until new waves of immigrants brought Irish, Italian, and Polish Catholics to the United States. At the same time there emerged alongside of the Protestant Establishment a new element, the "American Civil Religion," which assured a public recognition of "religion in general" in a pluralistic society. Because Christian-Judaic symbols have been used in each, the two have not been sufficiently distinguished by many people, including members of the churches.

In chapter 4, Mr. Arnold reviews twenty-two decisions made by the Supreme Court in areas of church-state relationships since 1879. The guidelines offered by the Court to provide a workable interpretation of the free exercise of religion implied in these decisions are identified and discussed in what is one of the most valuable sections of this book.

Chapters 6, 7, and 8 deal with three controversial areas of church-state relationships that call for serious consideration in current society. The first is a discussion of the question "Shall religious schools receive aid?" The second is a sensitive and compassionate consideration of the issue of abortion and conscience which has resulted from the Supreme Court's decision of January, 1973, that invalidated all state restrictions on abortion and gave the United States one of the most liberal abortion programs in the world. The issue is helpfully discussed from the point of view of religious liberty—is the father's religious freedom violated by his wife's right to an abortion? Is the family's religious liberty protected?

Is the doctor's religious freedom placed in jeopardy by decisions he must make? Is the taxpayer's conscience violated when his or her money goes to finance abortion under Medicaid? Did the Supreme Court's decision violate the religious conscience of a large segment of the religious population?

A third consideration deals with restrictions and limitations upon religion which recent decisions of the United States Supreme Court appear to have created—decisions regarding prescribed prayer and Bible reading in the schools, released-time in public schools for religious instruction, auxiliary aid for providing busing and textbooks to children in parochial schools, sabbatarian concerns, and tax exemption for religious organizations.

Arnold has produced an extraordinary volume in the increasing body of literature regarding the free exercise of religion. It combines, in careful historical perspective, a judicious review of Supreme Court decisions and a forthright evaluation of the vital issues of conscience involved. Few authors have provided in such limited space so profound and clearly expressed an analysis of church-state issues in a fresh perspective.

Robert G. Torbet

To Elizabeth

Acknowledgments

I am grateful to Jane Baldwin and Dolores Orr for typing the manuscript. I also acknowledge with thanks my debt to the First Baptist Church of Ann Arbor for time given me for this project.

Contents

1. A Little Slice of History

In the fall of 1951 President Truman appointed Mark Clark, a retired general, as his personal ambassador to the Vatican. On the surface it might have seemed a most normal and efficient thing to do, even though it was a more or less trivial appointment. The president recognized the Vatican as a small state and as a very important listening post in Europe. So it seemed to him, as it had seemed to Franklin Roosevelt before him, in the best interests of the United States to have a personal representative in that strategic and sensitive place. But the reaction to the appointment was furious. A virtual avalanche of objecting letters and telegrams descended upon the White House and upon Congress asserting that the appointment violated the historic doctrine of separation of church and state, a keystone in the arch of religious liberty, and that if consummated it would make a serious breach in the "wall" which "every schoolboy knows" has always existed and must always exist between the church and the state. President Truman was so impressed by the emotional furor that he withdrew the appointment.

Exactly twenty years later President Nixon appointed Henry Cabot Lodge as his personal ambassador to the Vatican, and the appointment was confirmed by the Senate with little comment and almost no protest. The event in and of itself is unimportant, except as it illustrates that a change of some significance had occurred to alter public opinion about the sensitive and delicate relationship between church and state. It may be that the American public had begun to grow up concerning the realities of being a world power in a dangerous world. At any rate, a lot of water had gone over, under, around, and through the cracks in the so-called "wall of separation."

What happened in those intervening years was as complex as any slice of history but perhaps more intricate than normal because of the acceleration in the rate of social change and the chaotic and violent social ferment which gripped the United States. Certain curious twists and turns in the legal and social fabric had created a new attitude toward church-state affairs. In the forties and fifties the busing of parochial school pupils was resisted with vehemence. Twenty years later the use of public funds for parochial school bus service is accepted without argument. Busing to achieve integration is the current hot issue. In the thirties and forties any kind of aid to parochial schools was considered unthinkable. In more modern times some form of auxiliary aid to parochial schools has been paid out of public funds in many states. A very recent Supreme Court decision, *Meek* v. *Pittenger* (1975), however, rules unconstitutional a Pennsylvania law which had granted rather generous supplementary help to parochial schools in that state and thus casts serious doubt upon the validity of much aid which is still given in other states.

Aid by the government to various religious projects, such as low-cost housing, retirement centers and nursing homes, colleges, institutional chaplaincies, etc., is now considered normal, natural, and constitutional. On the other hand, the Court has invalidated prescribed prayers and Bible reading as a devotional exercise in public schools as a forbidden establishment of religion. The issue of tax exemption to churches for their places of worship and education has long been a target for extreme separationists, and even many churches have proposed that such exemptions were improper, not to say unconstitutional. But again the Supreme Court recently has ruled that tax exemption for church property is valid and constitutional. In some cases the Court has ruled that the Sunday closing laws do not proscribe the religious freedom of those who worship on Saturday and make it only "more expensive" to be a sabbatarian. But another case has ruled that workmen's compensation may not be denied to a Seventh Day Adventist who refused to work on Saturday.

There have been in those intervening years bitter battles in some communities over the observance of Christmas and other Christian holidays in the public schools, while in other communities the issue has not been raised. Colleges and universities have generally increased their religious departments and activities, while at the elementary school level virtually all teaching of religion has been eliminated as a forbidden establishment, although the teaching of comparative religion is theoretically legal and is sometimes accomplished. "Released-time" programs for religious teaching have disappeared, one would presume by default of the religious enterprise, since they are still not prohibited if presented off the school premises. In general, the doctrine of separation of church and state has become blurred and indistinct, and at the same time, relationships between Catholics, Protestants, and Jews have never been more amiable.

In a period when some people have confidently announced that "God is dead," the Supreme Court has had more cases dealing with religious considerations than in all the rest of its history. The session of the Supreme Court which ruled against prayer in public schools was itself begun with prayer. More public money has gone into religious activities during the past twenty years than in all the previous years of American history, and yet religion, or at least the institutional church, is waning in influence and prestige and loyalty. These and many other anomalies are the ingredients which have given a new shape to American church and state relationships.

For the most of American history, church-state relationships have been viewed through Protestant eyes, with Protestant attitudes and prejudices dominating and informing public opinion and decisions. Protestantism earnestly and vehemently advanced and promoted the "no establishment" clause of the First Amendment, despite and perhaps because of the fact that a Protestant establishment had existed since the Republic began. There was a common-law marriage between Protestantism and the state, although its legality was carefully denied. The offspring of this union was the doctrine of absolute separation of church and state, which was considered to be imperative to religious freedom. A corollary doctrine, the sanctity of the public school system, went with the American way of life like shoes and socks.

Underlying the Protestant system was a changeless and enduring tension, not to say hostility between Catholics and Protestants, which could be depended upon to keep the home fires burning under the kettle of church-state affairs. The polarity between Protestants and Catholics was defended and excused as a necessary kind of challenge and response which, though ugly and intemperate at times, was inevitable and essential in keeping both sides honest. Protestantism was a constant challenge to Catholic foot-dragging on issues of freedom, and the Roman Catholic church challenged Protestantism to heal its divisions and make tracks toward unity.

One of the most radical critics of the Roman church during the 1940s and 1950s was Paul Blanshard, tireless high priest of absolute separation, who sallied forth frequently from the strong tower of Beacon Press to smite the Catholics hip and thigh. His book, *American Freedom and Catholic Power,* was for many years the textbook of anti-Catholicism, particularly for an organization then called Protestants and Others United for Separation of Church and State (now called Americans United for Separation of Church and State). Even the pages of the liberal and prestigious Protestant journal, *Christian Century,* were heavily laced with anti-Catholicism. The battle was joined in varying degrees of animosity and bigotry by the *Sunday Visitor* and the *Register* on the one extreme and every Southern Baptist state journal from Georgia to California on the other with a multitude of voices, mostly shrill, in between. It was out of this historical and hysterical ferment that the mighty flood of protest about his proposed Vatican appointment had come to Mr. Truman's "buck-stops-here" desk.

Catholic and Protestant tension, though ebbing slightly, continued until the 1960s when with the elevation of John XXIII to the papacy and the election of John F. Kennedy to the presidency, there came an abrupt and happy end to the quarrel. One of the chief ingredients of Protestant propaganda had been the alleged danger of a Catholic entering the White House as president. This was the last vestige of old religious restrictions on holding public office, which had resided in some state constitutions and had survived as a constant symbol of the fear of Rome which dwelt in the popular Protestant mind. This *bete-noire* had defeated Gov. Alfred E. Smith in 1928 and was a serious barrier to Kennedy's candidacy in 1960. The latter's forthright handling of the questions in a speech to a group of Protestant ministers in Houston did much to allay Protestant fears, but the issue hung ominously over the campaign until the end and undoubtedly contributed to the closeness of the margin by which

Kennedy finally won. But once the new Catholic president was inaugurated, the issue was largely ameliorated, partly by the charm of the young executive, and partly by the new administration's scrupulous allegiance to the doctrine of separation. When the pope did not move into the White House, and the sun and moon continued to shine, the ancient and ugly cloud of fear and suspicion was largely dissipated.

Far more important in the process of reducing Catholic-Protestant tension was the Second Vatican Council which was convened by the new Roman pontiff, John XXIII, who had succeeded to the papal throne upon the death of Pius XII. For four hundred years the Roman Church had lived under the mystique of the Council of Trent, which had been convened in response and reaction to the Protestant Reformation. It was certainly not the purpose of the college of cardinals in selecting as pope, Angelo Giuseppe Roncalli, a man of peasant background then seventy-seven years old, to update the Church and usher it into the modern world. Precisely that was in the mind of John XXIII, however, when in January, 1959, he announced that he would call a general council of the bishops of the Church "to open a window and let in a little fresh air." The note of reform and *aggiornamento* which was sounded by Pope John was met with approval and enthusiasm throughout the world, and though resisted strenuously by the Curia, it also found a welcome in the minds of a majority of Catholic bishops summoned to Rome in October, 1962.

Pope John died in June, 1963, the same year John Kennedy died, but Vatican II under Pope Paul went on to complete its work in 1965. It made changes in the liturgy, substituting the vernacular for the traditional Latin; instituted the singing of hymns, among which was Luther's "Ein' Feste Burg"; and promoted the reading of the Bible. The Council restored the principle of collegiality, whereby the bishops and the laity were given a larger role in the governance of the Church. Although many issues (celibacy and contraception, for instance) remained untouched and not all was achieved that some had desired, the Council made more changes and effected more reforms than anybody expected. No greater contribution was made than the openness and frankness with which the Council carried on its debates, and this spirit of open discussion was carried back into the churches and its lay councils.

The debate within the Council over issues of religious freedom was hot and heavy. Some of the bishops—certainly all American bishops—favored a position which would allow a strict neutrality by the state between different religions. What emerged was something less than neutrality but a strict departure from the old Trent and Vatican I dogmas which made the state a partner in protecting the "true religion." The Council decided that where peculiar circumstances in a country caused one religious community to receive special civil recognition, that is, a state church, the right of other religious bodies and all citizens to complete religious freedom should be acknowledged and implemented. Despite this special acknowledgment of state-church situations, the Council ruled that for Catholics separation of church and state should be the normal guideline of the future. Whatever the limitations of the final pronouncements of Vatican II, the Council's work began a new birth of freedom for the Catholic Church and the cultures in which it is dominant. It certainly had a profound effect upon the American church and its relationship with other religious bodies. Its impact upon American Protestantism was enormous.

The result of these two factors, that is, the recognition of full political rights for Catholics and the new freedom which Vatican II gave to Roman Catholics, has created a happy and long overdue rapprochement between the two major expressions of Christianity in America. Protestants have dropped many of their fears and prejudices, and Catholics from a platform of pride and acceptance have begun to enjoy their new liberty with gusto and enthusiasm. To a large extent, hostility and suspicion have been displaced by trust and love.

This is not to say that large points of controversy do not still exist between Catholics and Protestants, for it is obvious that they do. Many points of doctrine and theology are still to be, and indeed may never be, resolved. Doctrines of the church and the sacraments, papal infallibility, immaculate conception, the assumption of Mary, celibacy, ordination of women, and many other issues are still in contention. But there is a new open discussion about them and a recognition that Catholics themselves are not agreed on many subjects very close to the heart of their faith.

The more volatile issues are political and social, particularly the many issues which gather around the central problems of sex and marriage, birth control, and above all, abortion. But again, these issues, which will be discussed in some detail at a later point in this book, are now open for discussion. And with respect to divorce, birth control, and abortion, there is no more unanimity or consensus among Protestants and Jews than among Catholics. They are open problems of enormous complexity and dispute for our entire American society. If a new era of religious good feeling has been introduced into a torn and divided society, it has come because both of the two sectors of Christianity and the Jewish community are looking honestly and searchingly at their differences. They are also recognizing with hope and promise the vast and potentially healing areas of agreement which have always been there and are now being rediscovered.

Underlying the two obvious causes for this "era of good feeling" is a new recognition and acceptance of pluralism. America has always, at least in recent years, been comprised of three great expressions of faith: Judaism, Catholicism, and Protestantism, to put them in chronological order. Full recognition and consciousness of this fact, however, came belatedly to the American scene. When it did come in recent years, it came almost with the force of revelation that America is not a homogeneous Protestant nation. And its heterogeneity is not limited to the religious dimensions of society. A new appreciation for the rights of all minorities has burst upon the scene, spilling over into the religious milieu, and forever dispelling the myth of Protestant hegemony. Moreover, the element of secularization with its concomitant expressions of indifference to religious values, and particularly to religious prejudices, has given a new shape to religion and its forms and institutions, and especially to church-state relationships. What this new shape is and how it has found its way into law will be delineated further as this book progresses.

$2.$ The First Amendment

The first ten amendments were added to the main body of the Constitution almost as an afterthought. The Constitution proper contained no guarantees as to individual rights, an omission which seriously troubled Federalists and anti-Federalists alike. Thomas Jefferson himself complained of it from his diplomatic post in Paris. In order to secure ratification of the new Constitution, many promises were made in the states that various guarantees of individual rights and freedoms would be added to the document. And when the first Congress convened under the new Constitution, it set about at once, under the leadership of James Madison, to add in the form of amendments the guarantees which have come to be called the Bill of Rights.

It is significant that the first item in the Bill of Rights has to do with freedom of religion, and the thesis is sometimes advanced that the other rights mentioned in the First Amendment, that is, freedom of speech, press, and assembly, issue from the first and are dependent upon it. Whether or not that thesis is correct, it is evident that religious and civil freedoms are intertwined together, stand or fall together, and that free and democratic government is inconceivable without them.

17

The Constitution proper contains only one mention of religion, and that occurs at the very end of Article VI: ". . . but no religious Test shall ever be required as a Qualification to any Office or public Trust under the United States." This is not an unimportant step toward religious freedom in view of the fact that many of the colonial charters and the new state constitutions did contain certain religious requirements for citizenship, voting rights, and the holding of public office, and continued to make such restrictions under the new federal government.

It is the First Amendment, however, which carries the main weight and offers the chief guarantee of religious liberty. This guarantee is contained in sixteen crisp words: "Congress shall make no law respecting an establishment of religion, or prohibiting the free exercise thereof." The exact wording of this sentence, commonly divided into "the establishment clause" and "the free-exercise clause" was debated and altered extensively during the proceedings of the House and Senate, and its final form is the result of much compromise.

Every word of this familiar sentence is significant, and none more than the first word, "Congress." The main concern of the framers of the First Amendment was to put a limitation on that legislative body. The chief concern of the Federalists and anti-Federalists alike was to limit the powers of the national government. The necessity for a new Constitution had grown out of the failure of the Articles of Confederation, under which the new nation had successfully completed its rebellion from England. That Confederation and its Articles had been wrecked on the rocks of states' rights and sovereignty, plus financial chaos. The original colonies, now calling themselves states, were proud of their history and their origins, and jealous of their rights and prerogatives. They were reluctant, not to say afraid, to relinquish any rights or privileges to a national or federal government. The original Articles embraced and tried to effect a form of government which was a loose association of sovereign and suspicious states. Many of the people who had gathered out of desperate necessity in a Constitutional Convention to improve the form and substance of that government were still influenced by the original ideology of states' rights and wanted now to protect their states from encroachment by this newly formed Congress, of which they were members. Whatever power was given the federal government was conferred by the states, and powers not granted to the federal government were retained by the states.

Many of the colonies, and later the states, provided in their charters or constitutions for an "established church," that is to say, a church which was supported by public taxation, an idea not unfamiliar to any of the colonists. Several of these established churches had survived the revolution. Not only states' rights and sovereignty were in the minds of the men who wrote this amendment, but also the added factor of commitment either to or against an establishment of religion. Some saw the word "respecting" as a guarantee against establishing any national religion, or favoring any one denomination above another, and some saw the word "respecting" as a guarantee that the present establishments existing in their states should not be touched or tampered with. Some would like to have had an establishment of religion if it could have been their own denomination, but failing that, they were prepared to require that no establishment should exist if it were not their own.

Many of the original framers of the Constitution, influenced as they were by the Enlightenment, saw religion as a threat to the state, having seen and remembered the sorry pages of history in which the church by its union and entanglement with the state had exerted influence upon it which was harmful both to the state and to the church. Many of the colonists had come to America seeking freedom from the powerful influence that the state had exerted upon the church to the deterioration of both institutions. So the word "respecting" was a compromise which allowed old establishments to exist, but which prohibited the creation of any new establishment on a national basis, and which in view of the many and competing denominations and sects allowed each to exist without favor to any one group or combination of groups.

But with all that pulling and hauling between various factions and state interests, there was primarily and chiefly in the minds of the framers of this amendment the desire to secure religious liberty and freedom of conscience for churches and people. There had been no "Bill of Rights" suggested for the Constitution in the first place because the framers viewed the whole Constitution as a statement of "conferred rights or duties," and what was not specifically conferred was not to be allowed. No specific limitations need be placed on Congress since its powers and prerogatives could go no further than those specifically conferred. It was a widely held conviction among the framers that religion was beyond the reach of government and should remain so, and whatever the powers conferred by the people to their government, they did not include any interference by the state in the affairs of the church or in the doctrines or practices of religion. Religion was simply "out of bounds" to government, at least to the new federal government, as indeed were all matters of conscience, religious or secular; freedom of speech and the press; freedom of assembly; etc. When at the insistence of Thomas Jefferson and with the addition of the prestigious voice of James Madison, who had originally been opposed to any "Bill of Rights," the task of writing a Bill of Rights was attempted, the primary meaning of the First Amendment guarantee, after all arguments were over about wording, was to secure forever the right of churches and religion to be left alone by state and government.

But what of the converse side? Did it also mean that the church's voice and influence should be withdrawn from public affairs, from the society at large, and from the government? It is difficult for me to believe that this was in the minds of the framers as a whole, although it may have been in the minds of those most heavily embued with Enlightenment ideas and programs. The anti-clericalism, for instance, of Thomas Jefferson was well known, and some delineations of that will appear later in this book.

Our early forebears were convinced that the morality of a society depended upon religion, and since government could not exist in a democracy without a broadly based moral consciousness in its people, the presence of religion was necessary to good government. It was the purpose of the founders, therefore, to protect and foster the religious impulse and enterprise. To that end, generous tax exemptions were made to churches; provisions were made for chaplains in the military, in the Senate and the House; the words "In God We Trust" were engraved on coins; and a great number of public rituals and ceremonies were established. It is fatuous to talk of something called "absolute separation of church and state" when speaking of the First Amendment, for that amendment itself asserts that Congress shall not prohibit the free exercise of religion. The government is the champion of religion and religious freedom, not its enemy, not even a neutral observer or arbiter of its exercise. One would never dream of asserting that the government is neutral toward the freedom of speech or the press, and it is equally non-neutral toward religion and religious freedom.

Judge Joseph Story, a famous jurist of the early nineteenth

century, in his commentary on the First Amendment, expresses what was the common assumption of the framers and the populace at large—that government should support and encourage the practice of religion in every way that would insure integrity of private conscience. So far from being indifferent or neutral toward religion or wanting to level all religions, Story saw the government advancing the Christian religion specifically, preventing only a rivalry among the sects or the establishment of any one sect over another which "should give to a hierarchy the exclusive patronage of the national government."[1] Moreover, the founders, according to Story, were willing to leave matters of religion exclusively to the sense of justice of the state governments and their constitutions.

But Judge Story's commentary on the First Amendment, prestigious as it is among jurists, is not half or one-tenth as well known as is Jefferson's. If Story saw the government as the champion of religion, Jefferson, a man of the Enlightenment, saw religion as a threat to or an interference with good government, and for the most part it has been his viewpoint that has prevailed in American history. His most quoted commentary was Jefferson's famous letter to the Danbury Association of Baptists in Connecticut in which he stated that "a wall of separation between Church and State" had been built up by the prohibitions of the First Amendment. His exact words ought to be quoted:

> Believing with you that religion is a matter which lies solely between man and his God, that he owes account to none other for his faith or his worship, that the legislative powers of government reach actions only, and not opinions, I contemplate with sovereign reverence that act of the whole American people which declared that their legislature should "make no law respecting an establishment of religion, or prohibiting the free exercise thereof," thus building a wall of separation between Church and State. . . .[2]

Behind this simple metaphor of "the wall" lurks many a page of bloody history in which ecclesiastics assuming the scepter of secular rule had forced upon people and nations the doctrines of an ensconced clergy and had required their acceptance under threat of death and taxes. From this metaphor comes an anticlericalism which was angry and insistent in reaction to years of tyranny and persecution by established churches. Thomas Jefferson had drunk deeply at this fountain of rationalism which flowed from the Enlightenment of his day. His anticlericalism is clearly shown in his preamble to the Virginia Statute of Religious Liberty, which he considered one of his three most memorable contributions to history.

Whatever may have been the vagaries both in history and in Thomas Jefferson's fertile mind upon which this metaphor rested, it is extremely unfortunate that it should have been allowed to assume, because of Jefferson's immense prestige and the facility of his quill pen, the stature and force of law. For "the wall" is not in the Constitution, and it was created merely by a passing comment to a group of Mr. Jefferson's Baptist constituents. It was at best an opinion, at worst an ingratiating echo of the Baptists' own convictions. And since it is not law and has not the sanction of law, it is both surprising and distressing to find the Supreme Court 150 years afterward solemnly reciting it as though it were a statute. As Mr. Justice Reed said, "A rule of law should not be drawn from a figure of speech."[3]

Moreover, there was, even at the time Mr. Jefferson created this wall, a certain hypocrisy about it and about his use of it. For in the plans for his beloved University of Virginia, a state school, he had provided for a seminary for the purpose of educating ministers at Virginia's expense and had even inflicted compulsory chapel upon those poor fledgling divines. The plan, concurred in by Madison, was proper and in order under the laws of Virginia, but would it fit into modern interpretations of an absolute "wall" between church and state? It is apparent that even in Jefferson's day that imagined wall was as wandering and vagrant as "the famous serpentine wall designed by Mr. Jefferson for the University he founded," to quote Mr. Justice Jackson.[4]

What was Mr. Jefferson's real view of religion and its place in society? An interesting answer to that question and fresh insight into Jefferson's great and complex mind are furnished by a letter written to Dr. Thomas Cooper, a prominent British scientist whom Jefferson was wooing to the faculty of the University of Virginia.[5] The ex-president, who was then in his seventies, felt it necessary to explain to Cooper, whose religious views were suspect, that he might have trouble with some religious groups. The Methodists and the Baptists were congenial and harmless (Jefferson had tranquilized the Baptists with his letter to the Danbury Association), and the Anglicans (Jefferson still used the term to refer to Episcopalians) were similarly tame, seeking more from the state and the university than demanding of it. But the Presbyterians were "violent, ambitious of power, and intolerant in politics as in religion and want nothing but license from the laws to kindle again the fires of their leader John Knox, and to give us a 2d blast from his trumpet."[6] The Presbyterians were "anglomen" as well—that is, Federalists—while the Baptists and Methodists were "good republicans."

It seems obvious that Mr. Jefferson's views of separation of church and state were in many ways self-serving and that his notions of religious freedom do not in fact reflect the high and noble sentiments of his official rhetoric. He had a sectarian view of the church and wanted each sect to stay in its own backyard and plow its own corn. He commended those sects who agreed with him and did not interfere with the government or the university. He condemned the Presbyterians as "meddlers," which no doubt they were, and under our system of religious freedom, then and now, had every right to be. Apart from the arrogance of the statement to Cooper, it reflects an attitude of indifference toward religion, an attitude not uncommon among public figures in that day as in this. But the important insight is what he really thought about his "wall," and it is clear that Mr. Jefferson's measure of a religious group's worthy citizenship was calculated on the indifference, or approval, which that sect showed toward public affairs. If this be the kind of "wall" Mr. Jefferson had in mind, it is well that it never existed except in a figure of speech.

In all fairness to the great Jefferson it ought to be noted that he was in his seventy-seventh year when he groused to Dr. Cooper about the Presbyterians not being Republicans and thus opposed to his government, and that his bright views of religious freedom so crisply expressed in earlier public documents had become, as his hopes, his dreams, and his finances, somewhat diminished and tarnished in those reclining years. Having made that allowance for his age, one is still permitted to wonder if he did think of his "wall" as creating a watertight compartment which permitted the federal government no control over the church, but which also allowed the church never a discouraging word toward the government or the university. His ideal church, so it seems, was the docile church, fenced in well, and domesticated.

If he did think in those terms, he has many modern supporters and disciples, and that discipleship extends to the Supreme Court itself. Mr. Justice Frankfurter in a concurring opinion in *McCollum* v. *Board of Education* reaffirmed Mr. Jefferson's views and gave them contemporary coinage when he wrote:

> Separation means separation, not something less. Jefferson's metaphor
> . . . speaks of a "wall of separation," not of a fine line easily overstepped.
> . . . "The great American principle of eternal separation"—Elihu Root's
> phrase bears repetition—is one of the vital reliances of our Constitu-
> tional system for assuring unities among our people stronger than our
> diversities. It is the Court's duty to enforce this principle in its full
> integrity.
>
> We renew our conviction that "we have staked the very existence of
> our country on the faith that complete separation between the state and
> religion is best for the state and best for religion." . . . If nowhere else, in
> the relation between Church and State, "good fences make good
> neighbors."[7]

No stronger statement of the separationist viewpoint exists than
this, and it smacks strongly of the conviction that all ethical and
moral influence by the church, or by religion, should be resisted by
the state.

It is by all means important to try to understand what the
original framers of the Constitution had in mind when they wrote the
First Amendment, whether they were Federalist or anti-Federalist,
whether they were religionists or were indifferent to religion, but they
are not now with us to help us interpret and understand those
seemingly simple sixteen words. It is apparent that these two clauses
of the First Amendment regarding religious freedom, while not
contradictory, are certainly competitive. They work against each
other at many points, but if one clause dominates the other, the cause
of religious liberty is wounded. The two clauses are locked in a
creative tension. They do not permit easy answers of questions which
they themselves have raised. They clearly forbid an establishment of
religion in the sense that a Church of England is established and
supported by taxation, but they create and protect an establishment
of religion-in-general, or as some have called it, "an American Civil
Religion." This "common denominator" religion began as essentially
Protestant but has gradually expanded to include Roman Catholicism and Judaism. Do these clauses exclude the whole field of ethics
and religion from government? Are religion and government to walk
side by side through the years without ever conversing with each
other? Some undoubtedly would say yes, and others would deplore
such a circumstance as the very dearth of religion and the calamity of
government. If the clauses reflect the Jeffersonian view, do they
preclude the Puritan view which always saw religion and government

through the Covenant as supplementing and aiding each other? In a succeeding chapter, the attempts made by the Supreme Court to find ways to answer some of these questions are explored and delineated. But should the Supreme Court attempt to do so at all? What competency has any court to decide religious matters? How is the Court empowered to legislate not only religion but also morality and ethics by means of judicial review? All of these questions are before us in our day, and whether or not any answers are found, they ought to be continually asked.

One of the most important issues in constitutional history is how this First Amendment guarantee of religious liberty has changed during two hundred years of American history from a limitation on Congress to a general restriction applying to all the states. It will be remembered that at least five states, Massachusetts, Connecticut, New Hampshire, Maryland, and South Carolina, had established churches at the time of the writing of the First Amendment and thereafter, and part of what was meant by the language "Congress shall make no law respecting the establishment of religion" was to insure that these establishments should be left alone. As history would have it, they gradually withered on the vine, but they were free from congressional action by legislation as long as they lived. This really meant that the federal government for a great period of our history had no jurisdiction over the religious liberty of American citizens in the states. This may be viewed with alarm, and no doubt was, but it was also a circumstance which had a certain benign effect upon religious liberty. For if it made it impossible for the federal government to protect religious liberty in the states, it also precluded it from interference with the free exercise of religion in the states.

The Fourteenth Amendment, ratified in 1868, was one of the Reconstruction Amendments, by which citizenship and rights of the freed slaves were guaranteed. No person was to be deprived of life, liberty, or property without due process of law. Its provisions were obviously applicable immediately to former slaves, although one of the tragedies of our history is that it took almost one hundred years before this Amendment began to take its primary effect. But a secondary effect was to use this Amendment to make all First Amendment rights applicable to the states. The First Amendment which was originally a restraint upon Congress now covered the state legislatures and courts.[8]

It is certainly no accident that this action came at a time when the power of the federal government was being enhanced in all areas. It came when the civil rights of minorities were being flagrantly violated and the federal government was trying to respond to their complaints. As though by sympathetic detonation, the explosion in the civil rights house has set off similar explosions in the temple of religious rights. It ought to be noted, however, that the effect has not been totally salutary, and a certain officiousness by the federal government has worked against the free exercise of religion, as the power of the federal courts has overshadowed the local and state courts in the settlement of religious complaints.

3. The Protestant Establishment

The idea of establishment of religion, along with many other American institutions, began in Europe and was transplanted in the new land. It was in an effort to escape the repression of an established church that many of the early colonists had crossed the sea. Much of the motivation in uprooting themselves from their native lands was for those first settlers on the Atlantic seaboard the hope and promise of religious freedom. Most of this migration was Protestant, although the proprietary colony of Maryland was established as a refuge for Catholics who had felt the sharp teeth of Protestant persecution.

It is sometimes assumed that in seeking freedom from oppressive establishments the early colonists left behind them all notions of intolerance and persecution which they had learned at the hand of their tormentors in England, and that from the start the American religious experience was an experiment in, and indeed a crusade for, religious freedom. The truth is something considerably less than that. Several of the early colonies developed their own establishments of religion, supported by taxation. The Separatists, who had sought religious freedom for themselves and their children, steadfastly denied that right to others in the new colonies, while they assiduously built institutions of privilege for those of their own religious faith.

New England Congregationalism became such an establishment, based on the ideas of theocracy and covenant. While giving lip service to freedom and religion as a voluntary enterprise, these early Puritan divines constructed a closed society in which both the religious and the secular communities came under the same authority, and many of the expressions of their statecraft rivaled in cruelty and oppression any of the restrictions and tyrannies which they left England to escape. As the power of the new church-state increased, it was evident that the new ministers and magistrates were the same in persecuting zeal as the old bishops: The persecutions of Anne Hutchinson, Roger Williams, and John Clarke are well known to everybody. The tragedies in Indian villages stand as horrible examples of the failure of the new religious freedom. As our early fathers massacred the Pequots and others, they were sure they did the will of God:

> Unsuspecting, the Pequots were sleeping within their palisade at a spot near the present New London. Daybreak was glimmering on their seventy wigwams. Mason approached with his replenished forces in the night. His men rushed the wigwams and kindled them with torches. As the Pequots fled through the burning wigwams they were riddled with musket fire. "God is over us," Captain Mason shouted. "He laughs His enemies to scorn, making them as a fiery oven."[1]

In the proprietary colonies similar establishments of religion were constructed. The colony of Maryland, originally founded by George Calvert as a haven for Roman Catholics, reverted to an established Anglicanism in 1692, with subsequent disenfranchisement of Catholics. Pennsylvania, and its satellite colonies of Delaware and New Jersey, remained essentially true to their first vision of religious freedom, but even they required belief in God, Jesus, and sabbath observance for citizenship.

In many of the early colonies Protestant church membership was required for the holding of public office; taxes were levied for church maintenance; and each colony had its sorry record of repression and out and out persecution of Jews, Quakers, and dissenters, varying only in intensity. Only Rhode Island began and maintained a consistent policy and record of religious freedom.

Most of these establishments did not survive the Revolution, although Massachusetts and Connecticut and Virginia are exceptions. The state church of the Bay colony was not dissolved until

1833. Most of the state churches simply withered on the vine and were swept away by the new spirit of voluntarism, by the Federal Constitution, and by western expansion. Before they died, however, they left their indelible mark upon American society and history. In their place an inchoate and de facto establishment of Protestantism not only survived but also grew and prospered, insinuating itself into all the customs and habits of the new nation, bypassing the spirit if not the letter of the limitations of the First Amendment to the Constitution, which presumably proscribed such an establishment.

No plot or conspiracy to establish Protestantism as the official religion of America was ever mounted. It occurred quite unconsciously, for the simple reason that there was nothing to stop it. Almost everybody was Protestant, although actual membership in churches was less than 10 percent of the population following the Revolution. Of the three and one-half million people in the nation after the rebellion from England, only 20,000 were Catholic, and 4,000 Jewish. And though most of the three and one-half million apparently were not church members, they had embraced the notion of a "Protestant Christendom" without question. The wealthy planters and businessmen who took over the young nation after 1783 were the same people who had been governing the colonies, and they were Protestant. They may have assented to some particular denominational label, Congregationalist, Presbyterian, Anglican, or even Baptist, but they were all Protestant. The "doctrine of separation of church and state," to which all ascribed, was designed, so they took for granted, to prevent any position of privilege being achieved by one or more of the Protestant sects, but it had nothing to do with the underlying establishment of Protestantism which was the foundation of the entire religious enterprise. Baptists, for instance, who were staunch and determined in their zeal for separation, made no effort to disestablish Protestantism. Indeed, they would not have recognized that any such establishment existed. They did not want the Anglicans or the Congregationalists to gain the upper hand, for they remembered how rudely that hand could be applied to dissenters, but the unseen hand of Protestantism was friendly and benign and therefore not to be disturbed.

The Protestant establishment or hegemony had no sanction in law. The marriage between Protestantism and the government of the United States as well as the governments of the separate states, local counties, and villages was a common-law marriage, sanctioned by unanimity and homogeneity, custom and convenience, habit and history, and needed neither benefit of clergy nor a civil ceremony by justice of the peace. Marriages usually issue in children, and the principal offspring of this common-law marriage was the public school system, about which more will be said later.

The few Catholics and Jews in the new nation had something more than toleration, but it was not full religious freedom as specified in the First Amendment, or described in popular mythology. Freedom of worship, freedom to teach and evangelize, and freedom to build churches were afforded by the new nation to Catholics and Jews. It was always clear, however, that they were not members of the establishment. For establishment of religion always goes beyond the walls of churches. Specifically, it involves prestige, status, and the holding of public office. Some of the early state constitutions eliminated any religious requirements or qualifications for the holding of public office, but many baldly continued the Protestant proscription. Requirement or no, there were few Catholic or Jewish officeholders in the early days of the Republic, simply because there were few Catholics or Jews to hold office or anything else.

One can imagine many a political speech in those early days in which the prospective candidate boldly affirmed his belief in separation of church and state and thanked God for the Constitution's First Amendment which forbade any establishment of religion. And well he might. For he was, no doubt, a Protestant, though he may have belonged to or attended no church at all, and Protestantism already had all the establishment it needed. This was a very convenient, albeit unconscious, way of having one's cake and eating it, too.

An underlying core of anti-Catholic feeling had probably always existed in the English colonies. It came directly out of the English Reformation, the legacy of the grisly days of Henry VIII, Elizabeth, Bloody Mary, the Spanish Armada, and Mary, Queen of Scots. Protestant divines considered the Church of Rome to be the Anti-Christ and said so repeatedly. "Papists," as Catholics were called, were not only heretics but also something close to traitors.

With the coming of the immigrants, especially the Irish, in the nineteenth century, a target was afforded for all this pent-up hostility for Catholics. The Protestant Establishment was challenged economically, politically, and religiously. The first ghettos were Irish. The growth of Nativism which resulted in the Philadelphia riots, the burning of Catholic churches, and the coming of the Know-Nothings is well-known to history.[2] In New England, signs appeared on employment offices: "No Irish Need Apply." The growing fear and animosity which were being generated were expressed in names, such as Mick, Wop, Dago, and Polack. With the waves of Irish, Italian, and Polish immigrants the anti-Catholic sentiment ceased to be latent and inchoate; it was blatant and defensive. The politician in this later period changed his tactics to a shrill voice and direct attack. There was talk of vice in the nunneries, caches of ammunition stored in Catholic churches, and various "popish" plots to take over the government. Even into the twentieth century, the Ku Klux Klan rode at night and burned anti-Catholic crosses. And the establishment of Protestantism persisted.

I have listed all these negative factors only because this is a discussion of religious liberty. That liberty was seriously abridged for Catholics for many years. However, I do not wish to leave the reader with a totally negative impression of the Protestant establishment. It was a vast and grand system which gave cohesion to the fledgling Republic and which grew up with that Republic. As the Republic expanded to a world power of immense dimensions, so did Protestantism grow to be a "righteous empire," as Martin Marty has called it, with worldwide influence and proportions. Protestantism's religion was the faith of the nation, the glue that held all the disparate forces together. Protestantism's ethic was the mother's milk of capitalism; its conscience was the foundation upon which rested the public morality; its public school system was the lifeblood of democracy. It was a huge success!

Added to the basic Protestant sentiments and beliefs, sometimes vague, of the American people, was another element, often much stronger than any Protestant principle, which some have called the "American Civil Religion." From the very beginning of the Republic this religion took its place alongside of and complementing the Protestant Establishment. This civil religion, sometimes called "religion-in-general," was expressed at the outset of the nation in frequent allusions to God in the Declaration of Independence. In fact, the Declaration may be thought of as the creed of the civil religion. It was also expressed in the oaths of office administered to high officials, in the oaths sworn in courtrooms, in the establishment of Thanksgiving Day by presidential proclamation, the prayers of invocation in Congress and in the several legislatures, the inscription

"In God We Trust" on coins, and in numberless other less obvious ways.

The inaugural addresses of all the presidents express this religion in their constant allusion to God or the Almighty or to Providence, and the years have seen little diminution of that practice from George Washington to Gerald Ford. The Supreme Court, it is suspected, is alluding to nothing other than the American civil religion when it uses such terms as "Supreme Being," a term which is almost never used among theologians but has a lawyerly, Deistic flavor reminiscent of the early days of Washington and Jefferson. It may also be supposed that the Supreme Court when it says, "we are a religious people," or even "a Christian nation," is actually referring to the American civil religion.

It is only in fairly recent times that scholars have tried to separate the term "American civil religion" from the Christian religion, and the Supreme Court never has made any such distinction. One of the reasons the distinction was so difficult to make between the civil religion and the Judeo-Christian tradition was that the use of biblical symbols gave great symbolic power to the civil religion. The symbol of the Exodus, for instance, has been central. The symbol of the "Chosen People" and the symbol of the "Promised Land" were and still are prominent in the civil religion. In other words, the story was constantly told; the history was taught and recited of how the new Israel of God (America) crossed the sea (the Atlantic) to escape the slavery of Egypt (Europe) and the oppressive Pharaohs (the various oppressive monarchs) and under the providence of God established itself in the promised land (the North American Continent.) It was not only the church which was the New Israel, a well-worn doctrine in Calvinism, but also the nation, and this conviction has been a very powerful element in American life. Sidney Mead once wrote an article called "The Nation with the Soul of a Church," which expresses the core idea of what Americans have thought of their country from the beginning.

A well-developed hymnody gives strong and emotional expression to the American civil religion. The hymn "America," written by Samuel Smith, a Baptist minister who was a contemporary of Emerson, is perhaps the most important. Written to the tune of Britain's national anthem, not an insignificant fact, it has wrapped itself around the inner consciousness of every man, woman, and child of the Republic. The hymn reinforces the belief that this God of

America is the Author of liberty and by his almighty hand the nation exists. With the Civil War, the American civil religion moved to a new dimension of sacrifice, essential to any lasting religion, when in the "Battle Hymn of the Republic," young men were enjoined to "die to make men free." The familiar song "America the Beautiful" is a well-beloved hymn of the American civil religion and is often suggested as a more appropriate national anthem than the one we have. "God of Our Fathers, Whose Almighty Hand," written for the centennial celebration of the nation's birth, expresses everything that is great and good in the civil religion.

The civil religion comes well-equipped with saints. Most of the roster is made up of presidents, because the president of the United States is always the head of the civil religion. The shrines to Jefferson and Lincoln in the city of Washington are more than memorials. They are places of worship. Ezra Stiles raises George Washington to the level of sainthood, at least, in an expansive sermon preached before the governor and the General Assembly of the State of Connecticut in 1783:

> Never was the possession of arms used with more glory, or in a better cause, since the days of Joshua the son of Nun. O WASHING-TON! how do I love thy name! how have I often adored and blessed thy God for creating and forming thee the great ornament of human kind! upheld and protected by the Omnipotent, by the Lord of Hosts, thou has been sustained and carried through one of the most arduous and most important wars in all history. The world and posterity will, with admiration, contemplate thy deliberate, cool, and stable judgment, thy virtues, thy valour and heroick atchievements [sic] as far surpassing those of Cyrus, whom the world loved and adored. . . .[3]

The more familiar and less pretentious expressions of the civil religion are to be found in the ordinary rituals of the citizenry at every level of the common life. Every Kiwanis or Rotary club begins its proceedings with the hymn "America," pledges allegiance to the flag, invokes the blessing of the Almighty, continues with the communal meal, and goes forth to do good deeds of service in the community. The same pledge of allegiance was until recently almost universally required in public schools. Lodges, school boards, city councils, commencement exercises, and many other public functions are begun with prayer and frequently take on the shape and ritual of religious exercises. The Deity of this civil religion is often called the Creator, or our Maker, the Architect of the Universe, or Supreme Being, terms which are reminiscent of the deistic God of the eighteenth century.

But this God did not just wind America up and then go off and leave it. He is always viewed as present in it, its Preserver and Protector, the Lord of Hosts in all its battles. And the closing hymn at thousands of functions throughout the land is Irving Berlin's well-loved "God Bless America."

Although the civil religion has a distinctly Protestant flavor, it is readily accepted by Catholics, Jews, and especially by that half of the nation which makes no religious commitment at all. Cardinal Spellman in his day was a most eloquent and devoted exponent of the civil religion. The particularities of Judeo-Christian faith are often swallowed up, however, in a sea of "religion in general." The classic description of religion-in-general was provided by General Eisenhower who is reported to have said, "I believe in religion, and I don't care what kind it is."

In recent years the institution of "prayer breakfasts" has furnished a strong and subtle vehicle for the promotion and extension of the American civil religion. The prayer breakfasts are often attended entirely by businessmen, and a certain syncretism between the God of America and the great god success (called by William James the bitch-goddess of success) is evident. At one Detroit church where one hundred businessmen gathered recently, a General Motors' marketing executive solemnly described Paul as "the most dynamic, dedicated supersalesman of all." On another occasion in Chicago, a retired banker expressed the American civil religion, religion-in-general, and great god success religion in a nutshell when he said: "We pray for peace, and sometimes for the POW's and sometimes to do the right thing, because the right thing is usually the profitable thing, too. We want God to show us the right way to success."[4]

The national prayer breakfasts, begun in President Eisenhower's time, have insinuated themselves into the very heart of government, with presidents, senators, congressmen, and military types meeting regularly for prayer in the nation's capitol. The assumption of the prayer breakfasts is that the god of America and the God of the Judeo-Christian faith are one and the same, and that it is the business of that god to bless, honor, and sustain the prosperity and the arms of the United States. A sharp dissent to all this was expressed by Senator Mark Hatfield, a Baptist from Oregon, at the national prayer breakfast in 1973 when he flatly stated, "Events such as this breakfast contain the real danger of misplaced allegiance, if not downright idolatry. . . ." It was reported that there was a chilled silence following his remarks.[5]

Another auxiliary of American civil religion appeared when President Nixon organized regular worship services in the White House with the president, cabinet members, the military, and carefully chosen friends and advisers to the president in attendance. The preacher was carefully selected for his theological and political views so that seldom should be heard a critical word. The practice was reminiscent of the Old Testament prophets who were enjoined to bring a good word to the king. These services, now defunct, were saved only by their comic aspects from becoming a classic example of a prohibited establishment of religion.

To have a syncretism between the national state and the dominant religion is by no means unusual. Or to have a culture religion intertwined with the dominant religion of the country and the state is not to be wondered at. In fact, the wonder is that there has not been more of this syncretism in the United States, for, of course, every country of Europe and almost every country on the planet has made this kind of conjunction or union during all the centuries of Christendom and long before. The matter is worthy of comment not because it is unusual in history, but because it occurs in a nation which claims to have an absolute separation of church and state, even an absolute separation of religion and state. The American civil religion is a fact. It is not surprising that Americans should have a peculiarly American experience of religion. Dr. Robert Bellah, a sociologist who has "rediscovered the civil religion," is evangelical in supporting and promoting it as a desperately needed cohesive in a fragmented world.[6] From the point of view of religious freedom, civil religion is worthy of respect. It is in all of us who profess any faith at all. It comes under the protection of the First Amendment, and one may respect and honor it without making the nation an idol, without engaging in jingoism or chauvinism. But one needs to be aware of these dangers.

4. Decisions, Decisions, Decisions

If the Constitution is what the Supreme Court says it is, as one famous jurist averred, then those nine judges are not only the interpreters of law but also the makers of law. Thus we are obliged, even enjoined, to read their decisions, which for all of us who are nonlawyers is a most onerous task, if we are to know what the law is.

But not only has the Supreme Court become the interpreter and the maker of law, it has also become the arbiter, the interpreter, the maker of conscience and religion. The Court indeed would deny this and has often with appropriate modesty backed off from ruling on matters of religious doctrine. Nonetheless, it has on several occasions ruled on which faction in a church quarrel should receive the property, as in *Presbyterian Church* v. *Hull Church.*[1] It has issued many rather expansive statements of a general nature, such as "we are a Christian people,"[2] which must have worried Christian theologians, who have found little evidence of it, and Jewish theologians also, who, if it were true, would deplore it. The Court has ruled in theological areas of extreme subtlety, such as *United States* v. *Seeger* and *Welsh* v. *United States*[3] where it virtually equated religion and conscience.

Having said all that, however, we find it difficult to deplore the

37

intrusion or, indeed, to find any way to avoid it. For the Supreme Court for the last thirty or forty years has been ruling in the absence of any general consensus on values, which is in many ways the result of the advance of pluralism. Pluralism is a phenomenon recently recognized in our society in which a multiplicity of values and value systems coexist. Value or meaning systems have usually in simpler times come from the dominant religion of a society. Since no church or church group in America is sufficiently strong or influential to give to or impose upon the nation its particular value or meaning system, it has fallen to the government in recent years, and particularly to the law, and especially to Congress and the Supreme Court to provide a meaning and value system which will function as a basis for public morality. Since in our culture the law is closely associated with the common morality of the nation, the law and particularly the Courts have become in terms of that association, whether for good or ill, the expression of the dominant morality of the nation. Americans are prone to equate morality and religion, even law and religion. It is a natural step to bestow on the legal system the burden of defining conscience and measuring, interpreting, and even creating the religion of the nation. Two monumental Supreme Court decisions illustrate the process which I am here describing. The first was *Brown* v. *Education* in 1954 which ushered in a whole new era when it demanded that public schools be desegregated.[4] The second in 1973, actually two decisions—*Roe v. Wade* and *Doe v. Bolton,*[5]—limited the right of states to regulate abortion. The consequences of those decisions have only begun to be measured.

It behooves us at least to know something of these great decisions which mold and affect our lives in such a seminal manner. What follows is a brief review or compendium of some of the great cases, particularly those which affect the relations of church and state or religion and society. The review is by no means complete. There have been more decisions in this area of church-state relationships in the last thirty years than in all the preceding years of the Republic.

The Free Exercise of Religion
Reynolds v. *United States,* 25L Ed. 244 US (1879)

This famous case is the earliest test of the First Amendment limitation on the free exercise of religion. The Court reviewed the decision of the trial court in the Territory of Utah in which the defendant had been found guilty of violating a law, passed by

Congress in 1862, prohibiting bigamy. The Supreme Court affirmed the conviction. An act done under religious motivation (and it was mentioned in the review that the religious penalty might be damnation) was not to be sanctioned against the law and interest of the state.

It is perhaps gratuitous to comment that in the context of modern society with its penchant for serial marriage, the institution of plural marriage might not be struck down.

A distinction is made in *Reynolds* between thought or belief and overt deed; that is, the state interest has to do with deeds, not concepts or beliefs.

THE JEHOVAH'S WITNESSES CASES
Cantwell v. *Connecticut,* 310 US 296 (1940)

Cantwell and his two sons, members of Jehovah's Witnesses, sold books and played phonograph records in a predominantly Catholic neighborhood and were charged with breach of the peace and violation of a statute which prohibited solicitation of "money, services, subscriptions of any valuable thing for any alleged religious, charitable or philanthropic cause, from other than a member of the organization for whose benefit such person is soliciting . . . unless such cause shall have been approved by the secretary of the public welfare council. . . ."[6] The trial court convicted the defendants on two counts.

The Supreme Court reversed the trial court and ruled that the statute was in violation of the First and Fourteenth Amendments and upheld the fundamental rights to evangelize and disseminate religious literature and opinion by peaceable means.

Cantwell is also important in that it was the first religious case where the Fourteenth Amendment was incorporated into the First, thus making the First Amendment's limitation on Congress also applicable to the states.

Murdock v. *Pennsylvania,* 319 US 106 (1943)

In a case similar to *Cantwell* involving Jehovah's Witnesses, the defendant was charged a license fee under an ordinance of Jeannette, Pennsylvania, for distributing religious literature, either with charge or without. The ordinance was struck down as violating the First Amendment, an abridgement of freedom of the press and freedom of religion.

West Virginia State Board of Education v. Barnette, 319 US 625 (1943)

This was the last of the famous "flag salute" cases and a significant victory for dissenters of all kinds. A law requiring children to salute the flag as a part of regular school exercises under threat of expulsion from school for their refusal was declared an unconstitutional violation of First Amendment rights. It was a reversal of a previous Supreme Court Decision, *Minersville School District* v. *Gobitis.*[7]

CONSCIENTIOUS OBJECTORS
United States v. Seeger 380 US 163 (1965)

Seeger had been convicted in a New York District Court for refusing to submit to induction into the armed forces. He first claimed exemption as a conscientious objector in 1957, on the ground that his opposition to participation in war was due to his religious beliefs. He did not, however, claim any belief in a "Supreme Being" as required under Section 6 (J) of the Universal Military Training and Service Act which reads:

> Nothing contained in this title shall be construed to require any person to be subject to combatant training and service in the armed forces of the United States who, by reason of religious training and belief, is conscientiously opposed to participation in war in any form. Religious training and belief in this connection means an individual's belief in a relation to a Supreme Being involving duties superior to those arising from any human relation, but does not include essentially political, sociological or philosophical views or a merely personal moral code.[8]

Seeger's application for conscientious objector classification was denied in the lower court on grounds of religious training and belief, and particularly since he did not affirm a belief in a "Supreme Being." The Court of Appeals reversed the decision of the lower court.

The Supreme Court affirmed the verdict of the Court of Appeals, stating that Seeger's views were religious, sincerely held, and that such beliefs are a sufficient test for exemption as a conscientious objector. The Court found after careful examination of Seeger's theology and a considerable theological research of its own that an applicant whose religious view is sincere and meaningful and which "occupies in the life of its possessor a place parallel to that filled by the God of those admittedly qualifying for the exemption comes within the statutory definition."[9]

It is, at least, interesting to note that an amendment was made in 1967 to the Universal Military Training and Service Act subsequent to the Court's decision in the Seeger case in which the reference to a "Supreme Being" was deleted. This is the same "Supreme Being" which Mr. Justice Douglas once said was "presupposed" by all our institutions! (See *Zorach* v. *Clauson* in this review.) *Seeger* is vastly important in widening the view of "religion" to include moral and philosophical positions which are outside the traditional boundaries of religious belief.

Welsh v. *United States,* 398 US 333 (1970)

Welsh was convicted in 1966 of violating the Selective Service Law in refusing induction into the military. He appealed the conviction on grounds of conscientious objection to war "by reason of religious training and belief." But the Court of Appeals found no religious basis for Welsh's claim and affirmed the conviction of the lower court. Appeal was made to the Supreme Court.

The Supreme Court in 1970 reversed the decision of the Court of Appeals and validated Welsh's conscientious objector status. Relying heavily on *Seeger,* a very similar case, the Court carefully reviewed Welsh's views and statements concerning violence and killing and ruled that since his views were held "with the strength of more traditional religious convictions,"[10] his conscience would be violated by military service. While his religious training had not been all that formal, the Court ruled that the law required no more than he had to qualify as "religious training and belief" and granted the exemption.

Gillette v. *United States: Negre* v. *Larsen,* 39 US LW 4305 (1971)

Gillette, who was convicted in a lower court for failure to report for induction, and Negre, who sought discharge from the military forces upon receipt of orders for Vietnam duty, claimed exemptions from military service because of their conscientious objections to participation in the Vietnam war, which was unjust according to their contention. Exemption for those who object to any form of participation in military service was reasserted. But the two petitioners were denied exemption for objecting to a particular war only.

Religious Test for Office

Torcaso v. *Watkins,* 367 US 488 (1961)

Appellant Torcaso was refused a commission as notary public because he would not declare his belief in God. He brought suit to compel issuance of commission, charging that the state requirement violated his First and Fourteenth Amendment rights. The Lower Court refused to grant the license; the Maryland Court of Appeals affirmed the refusal. Torcaso appealed to the Supreme Court of the United States and the decision of lower courts was reversed on the grounds that neither a state nor the federal government can force a person to profess belief or disbelief in any religion. A religious test for holding office is unconstitutional.

The state is neutral as between belief and unbelief, and neutral as to religions which call for belief in God and those which do not. "Secular humanism" is called a religion, along with Buddhism, Taoism, Ethical Culture, all of which are groups which require no belief in God.

Entanglement

Walz v. *Tax Commission of the City of New York,* 397 US 664 (1970)

Walz, an owner of real estate in Richmond County, New York, sought an injunction to prevent the New York City Tax Commission from granting property tax exemptions to religious organizations for religious properties used solely for purposes of worship.

The Court upheld tax exemption for churches and religious organizations, along with all other nonprofit organizations. It appealed to history as its chief precedent, quoting Holmes to the effect that "If a thing has been practised for two hundred years by common consent, it will need a strong case for the Fourteenth Amendment to affect it. . . ."[11] The Court pointed out that not in two hundred years of history, during which time all states have granted tax exemption, has there been the slightest indication that such exemption points to an establishment of religion.

The *Walz* case introduced a new term, "entanglement," into the church-state controversy. Not to tax church property, according to the chief justice, would bring less entanglement between church and government than to impose such a tax. It was the first time this idea or doctrine had appeared.

Religion and the Public Schools

Pierce v. *Society of Sisters of Holy Names,* 69 L Ed. 1071 US (1925)

The Society of Sisters challenged an Oregon statute which required a child between eight and sixteen years to attend public school. The Oregon law was declared unconstitutional.

> The fundamental theory of liberty upon which all governments in this Union repose excludes any general power of the state to standardize its children by forcing them to accept instruction from public teachers only. The child is not the mere creature of the state; those who nurture him and direct his destiny have the right, coupled with high duty, to recognize and prepare him for additional obligations.[12]

This case established parochial and private schools as legitimate alternatives to the public school in meeting the state's requirement for compulsory education.

Cochran v. *Louisiana State Board of Education,* 281 US 373 (1929)

This case established the practice of a state furnishing textbooks of a nonreligious nature to children of the state whether they attended public or private or parochial schools. It was the first assertion of the child-benefit principle.

Everson v. *Board of Education,* 330 US 1 (1947)

This was a monumental case which opened up the modern debate on separation of church and state, aid to nonpublic, including parochial, schools, and indeed the whole complex subject of church-state relationships in a pluralistic society.

A board of education in New Jersey, acting in accord with a state statute which authorized local school districts to arrange for transportation of children to and from schools, had authorized the reimbursement of parents for money expended by them for bus transportation on regular buses operated by local transportation systems. Among those receiving such reimbursements were parents of Catholic children attending parochial schools. Everson, a local taxpayer, sued on the grounds that the state law and the practice were in violation of both state and federal constitutions. The state court ruled for the appellant; the case was appealed to and reversed by the New Jersey Court of Errors and Appeals.

The Supreme Court, with Mr. Justice Black writing the majority opinion, agreed 5-4 that the rebate to parents for busing to parochial schools was constitutional. It was important in that it was the first chink in the complete separationist armor and an assertion by the Court of the "child benefit" theory.

The decision was equally important in that it was, ironically, the first and strongest explication of the separationist doctrine up to that time and is often referred to as a precedent for the "absolute wall of separation" position.

Mr. Justice Black stated in no uncertain terms a position which seems to preclude any intercourse between the state and religion:

> The "establishment of religion" clause of the First Amendment means at least this: Neither a state nor the Federal Government can set up a church. Neither can pass laws which aid one religion, aid all religions, or prefer one religion over another. Neither can force nor influence a person to go to or to remain away from church against his will or force him to profess a belief or disbelief in any religion. No person can be punished for entertaining or professing religious beliefs or disbeliefs, for church attendance or non-attendance. No tax in any amount, large or small, can be levied to support any religious activities or institutions, whatever they may be called, or whatever form they may adopt to teach or practice religion. Neither a state nor the Federal Government can, openly or secretly, participate in the affairs of any religious organizations or groups and *vice versa*. In the words of Jefferson, the clause against establishment of religion by law was intended to erect "a wall of separation between church and state."[13]

But what the learned justice had given with one hand, he took away with another, and in precisely the next paragraph of his decision and with a few strokes of his pen he opened up the whole Pandora's box of ambiguity and ambivalence with respect to the language of the First Amendment:

> New Jersey cannot consistently with the "establishment of religion" clause of the First Amendment contribute tax-raised funds to the support of an institution which teaches the tenets and faith of any church. On the other hand, other language of the amendment commands that New Jersey cannot hamper its citizens in the free exercise of their own religion. Consequently it cannot exclude individual Catholics, Lutherans, Mohammedans, Baptists, Jews, Methodists, Non-believers, Presbyterians, or the members of any other faith, *because of their faith, or lack of it,* from receiving the benefits of public welfare legislation.[14]

The decision was also important in that it incorporated   the

Fourteenth Amendment into the First Amendment; that is to say, it made the First Amendment and presumably the doctrine of absolute separation applicable to and binding upon the states. *Everson* also set forth the doctrine of neutrality as a guideline for interpreting the First Amendment.

After allowing the rebate, which of course was an indirect aid to parochial schools, the decision closed with some eloquence: "The First Amendment has erected a wall between church and state. That wall must be kept high and impregnable. We could not approve the slightest breach. New Jersey has not breached it here." [15]

It is no wonder that Mr. Justice Jackson in dissent remembered Byron's Julia, who "whispering 'I will ne'er consent,'—consented." [16]

Engel v. *Vitale,* 370 US 421 (1962)

This is the celebrated prayer case which became a "cause celebre" for people on both sides of the question, which generated a great deal of heat and little light, but which showed how volatile questions of religion can be and how inadequate are courts to deal with them.

The New York Board of Regents in 1951 prescribed a prayer to be said after the pledge of allegiance in schools. It was not compulsory.

> "Almighty God, we acknowledge our dependence upon Thee, and we beg Thy blessings upon us, our parents, our teachers, and our Country." [17]

Not many school boards throughout the state decided to adopt the Regents' prayer, but one which did was sued by a group of parents charging that the prescribed prayer was a violation of their rights under the First and Fourteenth Amendments. The county court ruled the prayer was not a violation as long as it was nonsectarian and not compulsory. The New York Court of Appeals upheld the lower court's decision.

On June 25, 1962, the Supreme Court handed down its decision which was widely acclaimed as "a great victory" for civil rights and with equal vehemence was denounced as an act of treason against our heritage. Mr. Justice Black wrote the 6-1 decision forbidding the prayer as an act of establishment of religion:

> We think that by using its public school system to encourage recitation of the Regents' prayer, the State of New York has adopted a practice wholly inconsistent with the Establishment Clause. There can, of course,

be no doubt that New York's program of daily classroom invocation of God's blessings as prescribed in the Regents' prayer is a religious activity. It is a solemn avowal of divine faith and supplication for the blessings of the Almighty. . . . the constitutional prohibition against laws respecting an establishment of religion must at least mean that in this country it is no part of the business of government to compose official prayers for any group of the American people to recite as a part of a religious program carried on by government.[18]

The Court's decision was greeted with a furor which united in opposition such disparate voices as Billy Graham, Reinhold Niebuhr, Bishop James Pike, and James Francis Cardinal McIntyre. The matter came to its climax with the presentation of the so-called Becker Amendment to the Constitution which would have restored prayer and Bible reading to public schools. It failed of adoption.

As Robert Hutchins once said, "The wall of separation is strong enough to keep out a prayer but not strong enough to keep out a school bus."

Abington School District v. Schempp, 374 US 203 (1963)

The Schempp family, members of First Unitarian Church, Germantown, Pennsylvania, brought suit to test the constitutionality of a Pennsylvania statute which required Bible reading in the public schools in a regular morning exercise, which included recitation of the Lord's Prayer and salute to the flag.

The exercise of reading the Bible and reciting the Lord's Prayer was declared to be a forbidden establishment of religion in the public schools, a violation of the doctrine of neutrality. The state is forbidden to "employ its facilities or funds in a way that gives any church, or all churches, greater strength in our society than it would have by relying on its members alone."[19]

Mr. Justice Clark, who wrote the opinion, does leave the door open, or at least slightly ajar, for the study of comparative religion and the history of religion. He allows that the Bible may be studied for its "literary and historic" qualities, provided it is presented objectively as a part of a "secular program of education."[20]

Board of Education v. Allen, 228 NE. 2d 791, NY (1967)

The Board of Education, Central School District in Rensselaer and Columbia counties, New York, brought suit against James Allen, state commissioner of education, who had threatened to remove the school board from office unless it fulfilled the requirement in State Law 701 authorizing public school boards to lend secular textbooks to all children whether of public or parochial schools. The trial court found the New York law unconstitutional. The appellate division reversed and ordered the complaint dismissed, claiming that appellant school boards lacked standing to attack the validity of a state statute. On appeal, the New York Court of Appeals concluded by a 4-3 vote that appellants did have standing, but said that Law 701 was not in violation of state or federal constitutions.

The Supreme Court of the United States affirmed the New York Court of Appeals decision. The court said that the loan of textbooks to children attending parochial schools achieved a secular and legislative purpose, helped the state to perform its educational requirements, and helped children to meet those requirements. The law merely made available to all children the benefits of a general program to lend school books free of charge. Books are furnished at the request of the pupil, and ownership remains, at least technically, in the state. Thus no funds or books are furnished to parochial schools, and the financial benefit is to parents and children, not to schools.[21]

In response to the plea that Law 701 of New York violated First Amendment rights of appellant, the Court said there was no coercive effect of the law as it operates against him in the practice of his religion.

The real point of the case was the question of the choice of books. And several justices in dissent showed examples of textbooks which mixed religion and science and/or economics and/or history in a most ingenious manner. The Court dealt with this by asserting that the school officials ought to have sense enough to know a secular book from a religious book, and the Court assumed they would make a proper choice.

Lemon v. *Kurtzman,* 403 US 602 (1971); also *Earley* v. *DiCenso,* and *Robinson* v. *DiCenso,* 39 LW 4844 (1971)

Rhode Island's 1969 Salary Supplement Act, providing for a 15 percent salary supplement to be paid to teachers in nonpublic education was declared invalid in that it involved the state and the church schools in excessive entanglement.

Pennsylvania's Nonpublic Elementary and Secondary Education Act, 1968, authorized the State Superintendent of Public

Instruction to purchase secular educational services from nonpublic schools, reimbursing those nonpublic schools for teachers' salaries, textbooks, and instructional materials. The legislation was declared unconstitutional on grounds of excessive entanglement.

Committee for Public Education and Religious Liberty v. *Nyquist,* 413 US 756 (1973)

A New York law which provided three distinct programs of financial aid to nonpublic schools was invalidated as violative of the Establishment Clause. One program provided maintenance and repair expense of facilities and equipment for those schools which served low-income families. The second program provided tuition reimbursement to low-income families. The third program provided a tax benefit plan for the parents of children attending nonpublic schools.

Meek v. *Pittenger,* 43 LW 4596, 421 US 349 (1975)

The Commonwealth of Pennsylvania had been authorized to furnish "auxiliary services" to all children enrolled in nonpublic elementary and secondary schools meeting Pennsylvania's compulsory attendance requirements. Also the state was required to lend "directly to the nonpublic schools instructional materials and equipment, useful to . . . education."[22]

The "auxiliary services" included such items as counseling, testing, psychological services, speech and hearing therapy, and related services for exceptional, remedial, or educationally disadvantaged students, and "such other secular, neutral nonideological services as are of benefit to nonpublic school children" and are provided for those in public schools. The instructional materials included periodicals, photographs, maps, charts, recordings, and films. The instructional equipment included projectors, recorders, and laboratory apparatus.

Suit was brought in the U.S. District Court challenging the constitutionality of Pennsylvania's statute. The Court upheld the textbook and instructional materials loan programs and also the auxiliary services program but invalidated the instructional equipment loan program, because it felt the equipment could be diverted to religious purposes. The case was appealed to the Supreme Court.

The Supreme Court overruled the United States District Court and struck down Pennsylvania's entire statute, except for the portions having to do with loaned textbooks. The Court made its judgment on the grounds that providing auxiliary services and instructional material and equipment amounted to "massive support" to the religious enterprise, and its primary effect was to support a forbidden establishment of religion.

Released-Time Cases

McCollum v. *Board of Education,* 333 US 204 (1948)

Vashti McCollum, the appellant, charged that private religious teachers came weekly to the public schools for religious education which was substituted for the compulsory time required of students for secular education. It was therefore a violation of the First and Fourteenth Amendments. Children were excused from regular school on Wednesday for religious instruction on the premises.

The Court ruled that this practice in Illinois was a use of the tax-established and tax-supported public schools to foster religious and sectarian teaching and was therefore a violation of the First Amendment and the separation of church and state.

"Religious education so conducted on school time and property is patently woven into the working scheme of the school. [It] thus presents powerful elements of inherent pressure by the school system in the interest of religious sects." [23]

Mr. Justice Reed in dissent pointed out that Mr. Jefferson himself had initiated a similar system of religious education "within, or adjacent to, the precincts of the University [of Virginia]" and even included a system of compulsory religious worship attendance. Mr. Justice Reed, referring to the so-called doctrine of separation of church and state, made his rather famous remark that "a rule of law should not be drawn from a figure of speech." [24]

Zorach v. *Clauson,* 343 US 308 (1952)

New York City had a program permitting its schools to release students during the school day to go to religious centers, off the school premises, for religious instruction. This "released-time" program was privately financed. The religious instruction was given on a voluntary basis.

The Court ruled that such practice was within the Constitution and did not violate the First Amendment or breach the "wall of separation." The majority opinion was written by Mr. Justice Douglas who made several interesting comments:

The First Amendment . . . does not say that in every and all respects there shall be a separation of Church and State. Rather it studiously defines the manner, the specific ways, in which there shall be no concert or union or dependency one on the other. That is the common sense of the matter. . . .

We are a religious people whose institutions presuppose a Supreme Being.[25]

It was a statement of accommodation of church and state interests.

Mr. Justice Black in dissent saw no difference between *McCollum* and *Zorach,* insisting that "a wall between Church and State . . . must be kept high and impregnable."[26] Mr. Justice Jackson was offended at the decision, saying:

The wall which the Court was professing to erect between Church and State has become even more warped and twisted than I expected. Today's judgment will be more interesting to students of psychology and of the judicial processes than to students of constitutional law.[27]

Higher Education Cases

Tilton v. *Richardson,* 403 US 672 (1971)

The Higher Education Facilities Act of 1963 provides for federal construction grants for college and university facilities, excluding facilities used for sectarian instruction or as a place of worship or primarily as a divinity school. The United States retains a twenty-year interest in any facility constructed with funds under this act, and if violation occurs, the government is entitled to recover funds.

Four colleges in Connecticut, all with religious connections, applied for funds under the act. Appellants attempted to show the schools were sectarian. The Court held the act is constitutional and includes colleges and universities with religious affiliations as long as a legitimate secular goal is present and there is no pervasive religious atmosphere. It disallowed the twenty-year limitation, however, as a violation of the religious clause of the First Amendment, since after twenty years the buildings could be used for religious purposes.

Roemer v. *Board of Public Works of Maryland,* 44 LW 4939 (1976)

A Maryland law authorizes the payment of state funds to any private institution of higher learning within the state which meets certain minimum criteria and does not award seminarian or theological degrees exclusively. The aid is in the form of an annual fiscal year subsidy to qualifying colleges and universities. Suit was brought by appellants, four individual Maryland citizens and taxpayers, challenging the statute as violative of the Establishment Clause of the First Amendment, and claiming the four colleges, which are affiliated with the Roman Catholic Church, were ineligible under the Constitution to receive such aid. Because the District Court upheld the statute, the case was appealed to the Supreme Court. That Court affirmed the decision of the lower court on the basis of the provisions of *Lemon* v. *Kurtzman* that (1) state aid shall have a secular purpose; (2) aid would have a primary effect other than the advancement of religion; and (3) there was no tendency to entangle the state excessively in church affairs.[28]

5. Groping for Guidelines

Sixteen words, spare and weighty, carry the entire load of religious freedom in the Constitution of the United States: "Congress shall make no law respecting the establishment of religion or prohibiting the free exercise thereof." Congress, it might be said, has been faithful to this charge; and if it were left to that body, these words would still stand in their bare bone form in which they were born. But the Supreme Court has not been silent, although it remained largely so for the first 150 years of the Republic's history. In the past thirty years the Court has put much flesh on those bare bones, more than in all the previous years of the Court's history, not only interpreting but also actually making the law.

Not that the previous years had produced no religious controversy or violation of religious freedom, but the legal action had not risen to the federal level. In the early days a certain "looseness in the joints" was allowed for, and litigation and legislation concerning religious freedom were left to the states and to state and local courts. In 1947, however, the Supreme Court handed down its landmark decision in the famous *Everson* v. *Board of Education* case.[1] The Court almost casually and tangentially stated that the effect of the Fourteenth Amendment (no liberty denied without due process) was to make the First Amendment's establishment clause applicable to the states. In other words, everything had become a "Federal case." For years some state constitutions, for instance, had expressly prohibited the use of public funds to aid sectarian schools, and state courts had largely construed these provisions to prohibit free bus transportation and free textbooks to children attending parochial schools. With *Everson,* the state constitutions and state courts are overshadowed by the First Amendment, and it is this new development which has caused the many cases of religious controversy, particularly with regard to aid to parochial schools, released-time classes, prayer, Bible reading, etc., to come to the attention and decision of the Supreme Court.

Now, in putting additional meaning into those famous sixteen words, so succinct and beguilingly simple, and around which so much controversy gathers, the Supreme Court has been obliged to search for formulae and principles of interpretation with which to decide the specific issues of religious controversy which have come before it. No doubt the original framers of the Constitution could never have imagined how complex and wide ranging would be the Court's responsibility. But the Court itself is subject to all the changes and chances of history. As Mr. Holmes, one of the Supreme Court's greatest justices, said, "a page of history is worth a volume of logic."[2] The "wall of separation" had held up well for 150 years of American history. But almost suddenly, with the deterioration of the Protestant Establishment, the increased prominence of pluralism in the society, and the increased secular mentality of the nation, a plethora of cases challenging not only religion's privileged position and the Protestant Establishment but also the doctrine of absolute separation of church and state have appeared before the Court.

It might be helpful before considering the various guidelines which evolved out of the Court's decisions to recall again some of the dynamics which were present in the original Congress when the religious clauses of the First Amendment were written. There was present a faction who wanted to disestablish religion so that it would have no legal opportunity to corrupt the new and fledgling state. These people, indifferent or hostile to religion, were heavily committed to the Enlightenment and its anti-religious, anti-clerical, and anti-ecclesiastical bias. People like this are still with us now. There were those who, on the other hand, were apprehensive about the government's influence and power over religion and wanted to protect the latter from such corruption. And people like this are still with us. There was another unique faction which wanted to protect the established churches which already existed, had existed in the colonies, and would exist in the new states. At least five of the states had retained established churches, and the First Amendment was a double-edged sword to cut down any new national establishment of religion, but also to protect the established churches then extant. Probably such people are still with us today in the person of hard-line Protestants who would like to protect the unofficial Protestant Establishment which has existed in this nation since its inception. At any rate, with this kind of explanation (more lengthily delineated in chapter 2 on the First Amendment) it is clear how much controversy was built into these famous phrases upon which, let it be repeated, hangs the whole issue of religious freedom in our Republic.

No-Aid

It was natural that the first principle of interpretation or guideline should be the doctrine of no-aid, for it had been present from the beginning and for many years had no competition. It was the guideline of orthodoxy, resting behind the wall of absolute separation of church and state, secure and unquestioned, more an article of faith than a canon of interpretation. And in a simpler society, it had more pertinency than it does today since the church and the state are increasingly intertwined in many overlapping and mutually beneficial endeavors.

The first objection to no-aid is simply that it has never really existed in the practical relationship between the church and the state. From the very beginning chaplains were furnished for the military services and for the Senate and House and in most state legislatures. Church property has been exempted from taxation, which is a form of indirect aid, and in the recent *Walz* v. *Tax Commission of the City of New York* decision that practice which has existed since the founding of the Republic was confirmed.[3] Some support, direct or indirect, has been given to parochial schools and to departments of religion in colleges. The primary support to religion comes from the exemptions given for donations to religious causes provided in income tax laws.

Perhaps the greatest aid that churches and religion in general receive in this country is the protection which the secular state furnishes in many unspecified but no less significant ways. The churches enjoy police and fire protection, and no one would want to withdraw that from them, any more than from hospitals or libraries. The whole system of law gives enormous benefit to the churches and the entire religious enterprise along with the rest of society. Above all, the provision for religious freedom, which came late to the world and especially to Western civilization, and which is stated and secured by the First Amendment as the very first item in the Bill of Rights, is in itself a benefit and aid of incalculable worth to the cause of religion.

The other argument, no less cogent, which shows how inadequate and unsuitable the doctrine of no-aid has become in church-state relationships, is that it often hurts the religious enterprise when it is applied with a vengeance. It therefore cuts across the doctrine of neutrality. The slogan "no help, no harm" is often advanced as a rule of thumb for church and state relationship, but the truth is that "no help" often means harm. It was this fact which informed the *Everson* decision. Mr. Justice Black, who wrote the majority opinion in that famous case, began with a vehement statement of the no-aid doctrine, then turned abruptly from it to make the substantive decision in the case which was to award a rebate to parents of parochial school students for expenses incurred in busing their children to parochial schools. The Court's reasoning was that to refuse to provide busing for parochial school students when it is furnished for all other school children would be a breach of neutrality. To be sure, the Court awarded the aid to the parents, but there was no disguising the fact that the decision gave indirect aid to parochial schools.

This is not to say, of course, that the guideline of no-aid is without merit or emptied of meaning in church-state relationships. By and large, the government does not support or aid the churches in any substantive way, but when it does give incidental aid to the religious enterprise, either by indirect subsidy or by implied and inherent protection within a common environment which church and state share together, such aid is not to be construed as a forbidden establishment. Actually, in any absolute sense, the pressure of history has forced the abandonment of the no-aid idea. Moreover, the no-aid "guideline" contradicts the doctrines of neutrality and secular effect, which we will now discuss.

Secular Purpose and Effect

Closely related to the idea of neutrality is the doctrine of secular purpose, which has become an important test in church-state affairs. A governmental program which has a secular purpose or effect is considered constitutional, even though it may be in some manner conducted under religious auspices. Stated conversely, prayer and Bible reading in public schools present a forbidden establishment of religion since the purpose of such exercises is religious and has no secular purpose or effect. But the setting aside of Sunday as a day of rest, with the consequent inhibitions which are placed upon those who worship on Saturday, represents no forbidden establishment since the primary purpose of such laws has a secular objective, namely, rest and recreation for the populace. Government loan of secular textbooks for parochial schools does not represent a forbidden establishment of religion, since the secular textbooks promote the general secular educational aims of the state.

The most obvious objection to this doctrine is that the terms "secular" and "religious" or "sacred" have become increasingly ambiguous in our time. Churches are engaged in all manner of secular activities, and, in fact, the notion that the primary purpose of the church is secular has been advanced and supported forcefully in recent years. The church is engaged in the struggle for social justice. Would this engagement invalidate its tax exemption as a forbidden establishment? On the other hand, the state engages in various activities which are purely religious—furnishing a chaplaincy for the military, building chapels and maintaining a program of worship in military academies and on military bases throughout the world. It is supposed that in any ordinary use and connotation of the words "secular" and "sacred," these practices would fall under the classification "sacred," which, since they perform no secular purpose or effect, would constitute a forbidden establishment of religion. Should the chaplaincy be abandoned? One could go on and on with this game. To say the least, the guideline of secular purpose places upon the courts the unenviable task of making distinctions between the secular and sacred, which it is not qualified either by training or inclination to make, and which task in some related cases it has specifically eschewed. In this regard, Professor Kauper, in his Russel Lectures at the University of Michigan in 1971, has written:

> One feature of this problem is that the state brands as secular what the religious community labels sacred, and in the end the label fixed by the secular organs of the state is determinative. The Jehovah's Witness views the flag salute as an idolatrous and hence odious religious practice.

The state sees it as serving the secular purpose of promoting patriotism. Justice Harlan has suggested that while a program of released time for religious instruction for public school students should be held invalid, a program of released time for ethical instruction would be valid even though the teaching in some of the classes would have a distinctive religious foundation. Religious means may be used to effectuate secular objectives.[4]

Professor Kauper has further commented that all this suggests that while the courts profess incompetence to define and interpret religious ideas and practices, they indirectly do the same by giving definition to what is included in the secular.

In short, by a restrictive reliance on the doctrine of "secular purpose" as an authoritative principle for determining the delicate line to be drawn between the church and state, or religion and the law, the Court must come down on the side of the establishment clause, following the hard line of strict separation. To do so may ignore or shortchange the "free exercise" clause which guarantees freedom to take actions with a religious motive, but which may have a secular effect. Secular purpose is in reality a tangential expression of the separation doctrine that the business of the state is secular, the business of the church is sacred, and never the twain shall meet.

But also in following the doctrine of secular purpose the Court tends to cut across its own doctrine of neutrality. If secular purpose is the primary ingredient which validates government programs, is there not a consequent burden placed on purely religious functions, if those functions can indeed be measured and determined? Is the government neutral, or does it have a predetermined bias toward the secular and is therefore bound toward some kind of discrimination against religion? Presumably, under the secular purpose doctrine a church or religious body may receive tax exemption because it performs a secular purpose. But what if it does not show a secular purpose, and its function is purely religious? Would it lose the tax exemption? Or would the Court fall back on the fact that the churches are nonprofit organizations and are therefore entitled to tax exemption? What in this process happens to the religious classification? Has it no rights of its own?

Are Jehovah's Witnesses allowed to use a public park for some supposed secular purpose but not for the obvious religious purpose? And does not the government in its "brooding and pervasive devotion to the secular," as Mr. Justice Goldberg said, not only tend toward a doctrine of "active hostility to the religious" but also toward an inchoate establishment of irreligion? All the arguments which may be marshaled against the doctrine of neutrality as a guideline may also be directed to the principle of secular purpose and effect. But the secular purpose and effect doctrine may also cut across the doctrine of neutrality and make it null and void, in that a secular purpose doctrine, strictly construed, may add up to nothing less than discrimination against religion. And if secular purpose and effect is a constitutional requirement from the establishment clause, then not only is this discrimination permitted, but also it is required. The establishment clause has thus overpowered the free exercise clause, and religious freedom is threatened.

Neutrality

The idea of neutrality is on the surface a happy, attractive, and sufficient guideline. Who could be against it? One of the first and perhaps the clearest statements of the doctrine as applied to church-state relationships was made almost one hundred years ago by Judge Alphonso Taft, father of the chief justice and president, in an unpublished opinion: "The government is neutral, and, while protecting all [religions], it prefers none, and it *disparages* none."[5] Another succinct statement of it was made in the majority decision of *Abington School District* v. *Schempp* by Mr. Justice Clark: "In the relationship between man and religion, the State is firmly committed to a position of neutrality."[6]

The famous *Everson* case also used the guideline of neutrality, but with a new twist. After Mr. Justice Black in his majority opinion had paid lengthy and emphatic homage to the notion of absolute separation, as though, it seems, to convince himself, if not others, of his orthodoxy, he then proceeded to grant a rebate to parents for expenses incurred in busing their children to parochial schools. The rebate for busing expenses was made on the basis of neutrality. Not to rebate parochial school parents for this expense when all other parents of school children received it would be discrimination on religious grounds and, therefore, a violation of neutrality. The rebate was, of course, an indirect aid to parochial schools. It is apparent then that the neutrality guideline contradicts and makes invalid the no-aid classification previously discussed. It is also apparent that no-aid cuts across neutrality.

But is neutrality an adequate or sufficient principle upon which to base judicial opinions respecting the state and religion? It is, to say the least, a slippery and tricky concept. It is almost a non-word, which may indeed have abstract validity but, when it comes to application, is hard to hold onto. It is particularly difficult to apply as a working principle in the intricate relationships between government and religion. The free-exercise clause of the First Amendment is in itself a statement of non-neutrality. The government is not neutral with respect to religious liberty. It is an avowed champion of religious liberty so that non-neutrality is not only permitted, but it is also required. A state that is religiously neutral could not grant an exemption for military service on religious grounds, or tax exemption for houses of worship, or even furnish a military chaplaincy, or permit prayers in the houses of Congress. But neutrality cuts both ways. The religiously neutral state could not preclude aid to parochial schools which is given by the same state to all other schools. This would be discrimination based on religious grounds, and therefore un-neutral and unconstitutional. This point will be developed further in another chapter.

Is the state to be neutral between the claims of religion and irreligion? By insisting that a public education program ignore any mention of religion, or that religion taught in colleges is for a purely secular purpose, the state comes down hard on the side of irreligion. It would come down equally hard on the wrong side if it insisted, as some say it should, on a strict neutrality in race relations. To be neutral in racial tensions in our day, as it has been repeatedly shown, is to put one's weight on the side of the status quo. Not to be for is to be against. Not to decide is to decide. The very nature of the courts and the legal system is to make decisions, which, as every umpire knows, is where neutrality ends.

It would be fatuous to assert that the Constitution is neutral toward freedom of speech and of the press or other great human rights enunciated in the Constitution, meaning them no harm and giving them no aid. The Constitution of the United States is not neutral toward any of the cherished First Amendment freedoms. As for religious freedom, it is supposed to be its foremost champion!

Entanglement

Another guideline which has been advanced in recent cases before the Court is the doctrine of entanglement. In *Walz* v. *Tax Commission of the City of New York*[7] the main decision to continue exemption of churches from taxes, a practice which has existed since the beginning of the Republic, seems to stand on history. That is to say, with Justice Holmes, "If a thing has been practised for two hundred years by common consent, it will need a strong case for the Fourteenth Amendment to affect it."[8] That is the chief point on which the case rests, but Chief Justice Burger brings in the negative point that entanglement or involvement of a church in government or a government in the church is a situation to be avoided. And it is the Court's opinion that exempting churches from taxation avoids such entanglement, since to tax churches would involve the government in making appraisals, collecting the taxes, foreclosures, etc. In *Lemon* v. *Kurtzman* and *Earley* v. *DiCenso,*[9] on the other hand, the decision to invalidate Pennsylvania and Rhode Island laws which gave aid to parochial schools was based on the Court's concern about surveillance and inspection, measuring the amount of time spent on secular and sacred subjects, audit, and accounting procedures which would involve the government in the operation of schools. It was also concerned about creating political fragmentation and divisiveness on religious lines. All in all, the Court saw the state entering into the parochial school business.

Clearly this guideline is one of degree, since entanglement in some measure is a necessary part of life and history. The government of the United States always has been to some extent entangled in religious affairs. Chaplains in the military services, if it came down to a measurement, would have a hard time proving a "secular purpose and effect" in their labors or measuring how much time was spent on secular and how much on religious duties. The GI Bill of Rights was a massive entanglement of the government in education, and no restrictions were made as to where or to what college, religious or secular, the tuition was paid. It must have involved a considerable amount of "entanglement" to implement the system, but apparently the government thought the program was valuable enough to make the effort. If a law may be invalidated on grounds of administrative difficulty, it is easy to see how the entanglement theory could invalidate the neutrality guideline or the principle of secular effect and purpose previously set forth by the Court. It would go very well with the "no-aid" doctrine, however, because any aid in all spheres of life carries with it some kind of entanglement.

Child Benefit

This doctrine has been weaving its way through various

decisions of the Court since *Everson*. Direct aid to religious enterprises has been considered a forbidden establishment. But aid to children or to people directly, even though indirectly religious institutions thus may be benefited, has been considered constitutional. Textbooks have been allowed since *Board of Education* v. *Allen*[10] on the theory that such loans effected a secular purpose and aided children. The whole idea of the Elementary and Secondary Education Act of 1965 was to give aid to children of low-income families on the theory that such aid would break the "cycle of poverty." Recent cases, however *(Lemon* v. *Kurtzman, Earley* v. *DiCenso* and *Meek* v. *Pittenger)*,[11] have given almost a death-blow to the child benefit guideline.

Accommodation

Another doctrine or guideline, not so much stated or spelled out but practiced frequently by the Court, is accommodation. Many of the guidelines mentioned above are abstractions. They have validity, but their validity is limited. Neutrality is such an abstraction. The principle of "secular purpose and effect" is to a large degree an abstraction. Accommodation is what guides the Court when the abstractions play out their strings. The Court has often come to the end of the various abstractions and has accommodated itself to the needs of people. Interpreting that narrow line between the establishment clause and the free exercise clause of the First Amendment often resembles nothing more precisely than a high-wire trapeze act. Accommodation is the leaning and balancing you do to stay on the wire. An example is *Zorach* v. *Clauson*.[12] A previous case, *McCollum* v. *Board of Education*,[13] had thrown out released-time religious education as practiced in Illinois. The Court ruled in *Zorach* that released time as practiced in New York was acceptable if it were not conducted on school premises—an accommodation to different circumstances. The accommodation guideline, if it is a guideline at all, is the deciding of cases not on theory but on the facts and situation of each case. Accommodation is moderate and pragmatic rather than doctrinaire, specific rather than abstract. In the interest of justice, it seems to me to be the best "guideline" to follow, because it includes all the others but gives none an exclusive prominence.

It is clear that not one or all of these guidelines are sufficient to make decisions which are free from contradiction, so interrelated and intertwined are the considerations and functions of church and state in modern society. It is also clear that the thin line between the establishment clause and the free exercise clause of the First Amendment is hard to find, for the two are often competitive and contradictory in themselves. It is clear that the free exercise of religion may at times be emphasized to the point where a forbidden establishment of religion is formed. It is also clear that the establishment of religion clause may be so narrowly interpreted as to infringe upon the free exercise of religion. But is it not true that the protection and, shall we say, friendship which the Constitution requires the state to give the religious enterprise is in itself a form of establishment? For while the Constitution proscribes the establishment of any one church or any combination of churches, it also requires that the state maintain a benign interest in religious freedom and in doing that it becomes the friend of religion and certainly not its enemy.

Postscript

The Tax Reform Act of 1969 carried a provision that religious organizations beginning in 1975 should submit annual reports of their operations to the Internal Revenue Service (Form 990), excepting only those organizations which qualify under the rubric of "integrated auxiliaries of a church." The form calls for a detailed financial report and is apparently conceived to divulge any "unrelated business income," which might be subject to taxation. It may be said that the IRS, always on the lookout for a broader tax base, is not without justification in its search for such income in church organizations. When a church is in the girdle business or has a string of wineries, or is even engaged in bingo games, it may expect to find the IRS lurking in the shadows, and rightly so.

However, the IRS, which has its power from Congress, has recently given rather narrow limitations and restrictions as to which organizations shall be exempt from filing these forms, and a considerable controversy has developed over the definition of an "integrated auxiliary." The IRS has defined such an auxiliary as an "organization . . . whose primary purpose is to carry out the tenets, functions, and principles of faith of the church with which it is affiliated. . . ."[14] This definition, the IRS further explains, does not include hospitals, orphanages, homes for the elderly, or nursing homes, all of which are the traditional and biblical arms of the church. It does include a youth organization, a men's fellowship, an elementary parochial school, a seminary, but not a college which offers general education. This is not to say that any of these church organizations which do not qualify as "integrated auxiliaries" are necessarily subject to taxation, for they are tax-exempt under the more general classification of nonprofit organizations, but it does mean that the IRS is taking it upon itself to define which functions of the church are "religious" and which are "secular," a distinction that is increasingly unclear in our world but is certainly not within the scope of the government's taxing agency to define. When the government seeks to define the mission of the church, it is obviously limiting the church and is putting itself in a position to judge, interfere with, and restrict the church's operations.

This controversy has not reached the point of litigation, but it seems obvious that when it does, the IRS will find itself in conflict with the various Supreme Court decisions which have forbidden "entanglement," and also with the guideline of "secular purpose and effect." It seems as though the IRS is trying to turn back the clock to confine the church to obviously religious concerns, ignoring the fact that the church has always been engaged in "secular" activities, and many of those activities have been and are the central expression of its faith. The IRS ignores the fact that the Supreme Court has given its blessing to the church's secular activities and has even prescribed aid from the state, rather than penalty, for precisely those operations which have a secular purpose and effect. It looks like a stormy time ahead and a lot more work for lawyers. But as long as the First Amendment obtains, and the fundamental principle is remembered that it is the business of the government, except in cases of actual violation of law, to leave religion alone, one may be allowed to be sanguine of the end result.

6. Shall Religious Schools Receive Aid?

Education and religion have accompanied each other through the centuries, sometimes as enemies, but more often as friends. In America formal education began in the churches of the early colonies. The parson was often the schoolmaster. It was not until the early nineteenth century that a system of public schools was gradually developed. A part of the American dream was that every boy and girl in the land should be afforded a free education. The public schools soon became the chief meaning system, the glue and the cherished hope of democracy, the pride and glory of the nation.

The overwhelming Protestant complexion of the nation made it possible to permit teaching with considerable religious content in the schools. There was no uniformity about religious influence, and it was not usually sectarian. Some schools were almost totally secular. But in many localities the Christian festivals were celebrated, often, as the years went by, accompanied by a similar observation of Jewish holidays. By and large there was toleration and appreciation of both religions. The public school teachers were not the teachers of religion, but they were usually religious people and were friendly and not hostile to the religious enterprise. Prayers and Bible reading were the common and habitual occurrences in some classrooms and were not forbidden where the teacher wished to conduct such exercises.

Only in recent years have the hard-line separationists been able to root out all religious observances, or even the flavor of religion, from public schools; although to be strictly accurate, it is "prescribed prayers" which are forbidden, leaving the door ajar, one presumes, for private or spontaneous prayer. And in further service of accuracy, it is Bible reading as a devotional exercise which is proscribed, and not the reading of the Bible as literature. With those two qualifications, it is still valid to say that religion is largely excluded from the public schools of America. Curiously, this achievement for a nation devoted to religious freedom has been reached in the name of religious freedom, as equal protection for the rights of religious as well as irreligious people. Since religious freedom has been thought to depend upon absolute separation of church and state, now that the public schools have become absolutely secular, the event is hailed by secularists and by many religionists as a singular victory for freedom—and even more curious, for faith. Many religious people view it as disaster.

Early in American history, especially with the coming of the immigrants in the nineteenth century, parochial schools were established. They were largely Roman Catholic. They were conceived in dissent and born of reaction. Although the Protestant school system was predominantly secular, it had just enough of a religious flavor to satisfy Protestants and alienate Roman Catholics. The parochial schools became a haven and a refuge from a hostile Protestant society. The parochial school also preserved something of the old ethnic background, Irish, German, Italian, or French, which had been left behind.

The parochial school system was also an instrument of evangelism, nurture, and continuity for Roman Catholics. "Train up a child in the way he should go . . ." (Proverbs 22:6) was the underlying foundation and creative impulse of this impressive and fast-growing parochial school program. The Protestant establishment looked askance at these schools, not only with condescension, for Protestants considered them inferior and foreign, but also with a touch of envy and apprehension. Americans have always had an unfortunate penchant for believing two rather odd theories of history—the "conspiracy" theory, and the "devil" theory. Both theories have been employed to discredit the Catholic church and its parochial school system.

Parochial schools, mainly Roman Catholic, were supported out of parish funds, although some schools were administered and supported by a diocese or a teaching order. Whatever their administration the cost of parochial schools was privately borne. Catholic parents were fiercely loyal in underwriting their schools out of meager earnings. If they were property owners, these Catholic parents were obliged also to support the public schools. Such a double burden was possible to bear only because of the sacrifice and devotion of the religious orders who comprised the faculties of the schools. For 140 years it was the sacrificial lives of these nuns and teaching brothers, in addition to the priests, who formed the foundation of the Roman Catholic Church in America.

In the last twenty years, with rising costs in all education, and with the decline in the number of young women who are entering the teaching orders, a controversy of increasing intensity has developed in the nation over parochial schools. The controversy is not only Protestant-Catholic in dimension, but it is also religious-secular since all religious content has been eliminated from public schools. It is a controversy which rages in the Roman Catholic Church itself. Some Catholics would reduce their schools to include only the elementary grades. Others want to eliminate them entirely. Some hold out for a "shared time" plan whereby Catholic students would attend the public schools for all secular courses and attend the parochial schools only for religious instruction. Many Catholic schools have been closed during the past ten years. The controversy rages also in various sects of Protestantism over the "godless" public schools, and many Protestant parochial schools have sprung up in recent years to provide an alternative.

It may be helpful to get some perspective at this point on the number and kinds of schools, their enrollment, and the comparison of those figures with public school enrollment:

Enrollment in public and nonpublic Schools—1974–75 [1]

Public Schools	45,486,292

Nonpublic Schools	
Roman Catholic	3,614,000
Nat'l Ass'n of Independents	258,100
Lutheran	214,000
Jewish	89,700
Seventh-day Adventists	73,869
Episcopal	65,100

Nat'l Union of Christian Schools (Christian Reformed)	62,800	
Nat'l Ass'n of Christian Schools	57,400	
Friends (Quakers)	14,600	
Misc. (Black Muslims, H. Krishna etc.)	50,000	
Total Nonpublic		4,499,569
Total Enrollment All Schools		49,985,861

The first Catholic president, John F. Kennedy, was careful to affirm his belief in an absolute separation of church and state which precluded any and all aid to parochial schools. Lyndon B. Johnson, coming to the presidency upon the death of Kennedy, and freed from the political pressures of his Catholic predecessor, gave strong backing to both public and nonpublic schools. He was joined in seeking and getting such aid by the National Council of Churches and the National Education Association. Although both of those bodies saw the main issue as directing aid to children in lower and lower middle income groups, not aid to parochial schools, they were following the logic of *Everson* v. *Board or Education,* [2] that to aid some children while denying aid to others because of their religion was a violation of neutrality.

The movement proceeded, not without controversy, until in 1965 it peaked with the passage of the Elementary and Secondary Education Act, which gave federal aid to public and nonpublic schools. ESEA was designed to give aid primarily to schools serving low and middle income groups.

In the campaign of 1968 Richard Nixon promised more aid to parochial schools; and when he became president, he invited Roman Catholic prelates and educators to the White House for a parley on their financial problems. Mr. Nixon also formed a President's Commission on School Finance that would consider the plight of parochial schools. The Nixon administration also announced that it was considering a voucher plan whereby parents would receive from the government tuition vouchers which could be used in any school, public, private, or parochial. Schools were to be reimbursed in the amount of the vouchers they had received from parents.

To make legal in the states the ample funds which were flowing from Washington, the various legislatures passed laws giving sanction to "parochiaid." Pennsylvania, for instance, passed a quite liberal parochiaid statute in 1968. On the other hand, Michigan a year later passed a very stringent law which largely proscribed any aid to parochial schools. Similar expressions of "aid" and "no-aid" to parochial schools were written into law throughout the nation. Powerful arguments on both sides of the question have been advanced.

The Arguments for Parochiaid

(1) Parochial schools have a legitimate reason for existence, and when they meet all state and federal educational requirements, they are a fulfillment of the requirements made by the states for compulsory education.

(2) Education without religion, and especially if the qualifier "without religion" carries with it a definite bias against religion, is inadequate education. Such a system and such a bias establish "secular humanism" as the state-supported religion of the nation.

(3) Parents who wish to send their children to parochial schools should be able to do so without financial penalty. To require parents to support the public schools by taxation and to be prevented from sending their children to parochial schools of choice because of financial hardship is to discriminate against such parents and their children because of their religion. Such practice is a violation of the First and Fourteenth Amendments, an abridgment of free-exercise and equal-protection rights. Some support, then, of parochial schools is not only *not* forbidden, but it is also required.

(4) Parochial schools are a legitimate alternative to public schools. The religious dimension adds a quality to the education of children. Parochial schools furnish variety and enrichment of curriculum and promote pluralism. Since public schools are a virtual monopoly, they could do with some competition, for their own sakes and the consequent improvement of all schools in quality education.

(5) Parochial schools represent a saving to taxpayers. If the parochial schools should fail, the full load of parochial school student enrollment pouring into public schools would result in immense problems and expense.

The Arguments Against Parochiaid

(1) Parochial schools are religious institutions, usually a part of a particular church. To support them is to subsidize that church and is, therefore, a violation of the establishment clause of the First

Amendment and the espoused doctrine of church-state separation.

(2) Aid to parochial schools would be a massive expense to taxpayers, far in excess of any saving which might be involved. Support for parochial schools would make for a proliferation of many kinds of religious schools, a "balkanization," as it were, which would be costly and nonproductive in quality education. Also such massive support to religious schools might destroy, or at least enfeeble, the public school system.

(3) If the government subsidizes parochial schools, it must inevitably control them. Such control would constitute a forbidden "entanglement" of religion and government.

(4) Public support of parochial schools would lead to religious, class, and racial segregation. Parochial schools are now being used by some to avoid integration, and public support would put a stamp of approval on such a practice.

(5) Rather than promote pluralism, parochiaid would advance and foster a narrow sectarian homogeneity. The public schools, on the other hand, give to education and culture a broad, pluralistic richness and appreciation of many and all religions, thus leading to understanding and harmony in the society.

(6) The charge that public schools, comprised as they presently are of Protestants, Jews, Roman Catholics, Orthodox, and many other sects, form another "religion" or the establishment of irreligion is patently absurd.

It might be added that both sides in this debate have been accused of "dumping" their incorrigibles on the other. Both sides are accused of promoting segregation. The parochial schools are more culpable in the latter point, although recent laws forbid segregation in all schools. The principle charge against public schools is that children learn racial hatred in their classrooms, halls, playgrounds, and especially in their restrooms.

The Continuing Debate

Public school educators and large segments of the general public have proceeded from the beginning of the Republic under the assumption that the public school system, which was an expression of the original Protestant establishment, is the unifying and cohering instrument of American democracy. The public schools were the teachers of democracy. If there were to be an assimilation of the alien elements which the immigrants represented, the institution of public education nominated itself to be that assimilator or "melting pot." The Nativists, we remember, who were most blatant in their anti-Catholicism during the nineteenth century, advanced their cause more on the charge that Catholics were "un-American" than that they were "unchristian." Although so prestigious an educator as James B. Conant, president of Harvard, would have eschewed any connection with nineteenth-century Nativism, he still stated its basic tenet far into the twentieth century: ". . . The greater the proportion of our youth who fail to attend our public schools and who receive their education elsewhere, the greater the threat to our democratic unity. To use taxpayers' money to assist private schools is to suggest that American society use its own hands to destroy itself." [3] Will Herberg's wry response to this rather surprising remark by Dr. Conant is to the point: "If private schools are really such a menace to American democratic society, they should not merely be denied public funds, they should be outlawed."[4]

How very important then was the Supreme Court's decision in *Pierce* v. *Society of Sisters,*[5] which, despite Mr. Conant, had brought a new freedom and official recognition to the parochial and private school. In fact, *Pierce* has been hailed as a virtual Magna Charta not only for private schools but also for parents. What *Pierce* established was the American principle that the education of children lay, at bottom, not in the hands of the state or even in the hands of educators, but in the hands of parents. Education is too serious a matter to be turned over to the state or to the schools.

The process of judicial review has gone on from *Pierce* in a winding and sometimes bewildering manner. With *Everson* v. *Board of Education*[6] in 1947, Mr. Justice Black handed down his astonishing decision which granted a rebate to parochial school parents for expenses incurred in busing their children to school, and it was a decision which filled the separationists with consternation.

It was a small concession to the needs of parochial school children, but it was something. *McCollum* v. *Board of Education*[7] came along as a backward step to religious freedom in 1948 when all released-time education was ruled to be a forbidden establishment. Then, in 1952, *Zorach* v. *Clauson*[8] partially reversed *McCollum* when it was allowed that released-time religious education might be conducted off the public school premises. Next, came *Board of Education* v. *Allen*[9] which authorized the free "loan" of textbooks to students attending parochial schools.

With the passage of the 1965 Elementary and Secondary Education Act, substantial amounts of money began to flow to help parochial schools, even in some cases for the payment of teachers' salaries. But the Court in *Lemon* v. *Kurtzman*[10] and *Earley* v. *DiCenso*[11] struck down Pennsylvania and Rhode Island statutes which had permitted aid to parochial schools in those states. The decision was made on the ground that such aid constituted unlawful "entanglement" between church and state. In 1975 in another Pennsylvania case, *Meek* v. *Pittenger,*[12] the Court invalidated almost all of a Pennsylvania statute which had authorized auxiliary aid to parochial schools. Only the section of the law which granted textbook loans to parochial school pupils was retained. The kinds of "auxiliary" aid which *Meek* proscribes are psychological testing, speech therapy, nursing care and other medical aid, and special education for handicapped children. At this stage, one might ask, "Is education too serious a matter to be left to the Supreme Court?"

But there was more. A recent decision in a Federal District Court in New York[13] banned cost reimbursement to parochial schools for state-required attendance and test reporting. At the same time other private schools which charge large tuition fees for students are reimbursed for the cost of fulfilling state requirements of attendance and test reporting. The pastor of the parish rightly protests this kind of flagrant discrimination:

> St. Joseph's of Yorkville School, with a base tuition rate of $180 a year, serving families of low and moderate income, is denied the modest reimbursement of our costs to file state-required reports, while a non-sectarian private school, an intervenor-defendant in this case, with a tuition of $2,750 a year, serving high income people, continues to receive its reimbursement.[14]

While all this was going on to prevent any trickle of aid to reach parochial schools, another process was proceeding to remove all traces of religion from public schools. *McCollum* made released-time religious education on public school premises a forbidden establishment. In *Abington School District* v. *Schempp,*[15] Bible reading as a religious exercise was prohibited in public schools. In *Engel* v. *Vitale,*[16] all prescribed prayers were excluded. The effect of these cases and the general trend to forbid all religious ceremonies and observances was to make the public schools entirely secular.

The Court has disregarded in the parochial school issue its own guidelines of secular purpose and effect. The secular purpose of parochial schools is apparent since the overwhelming amount of time spent in a parochial school classroom is concerned with secular subjects. Secular education is compulsory in the United States. It is required by law that every property owner support the public schools through taxation. Since public education is heavily supported by the federal government, all who pay *income* taxes are also required to support the public schools. Some parents, Protestant, Catholic, and Jewish, choose to meet the state's compulsory education requirement for their children (and they bear the primary responsibility for their children's education) by sending them to parochial schools. If the federal government refuses to provide any aid to parochial schools, which are helping parents to fulfill the compulsory education requirement—a secular purpose and effect if there ever was one—the Court is by this means creating an unnecessary and unfair hardship for parochial school parents.

The Court is also disregarding its guideline of child benefit. Under the ESEA of 1965, large amounts of federal money are going into schools. The act was designed to help lower income people, and all manner of services are provided to schools which otherwise, it is assumed, could not afford them. These services include various medical benefits, special kinds of education for the handicapped, speech therapy, etc. These funds go to private schools as well as public, some of which charge a considerable tuition fee, as in the Yorkville (N.Y.C.) school case previously cited. But the same funds are denied parochial schools. The only conclusion one can draw is that the state wishes to discriminate against children on account of their religious affiliation.

It is almost too obvious to say that the Court is also by this action violating its own doctrine of neutrality. If neutrality is to be summed up in the aphorism "help none; harm none," it is apparent that the statement is made meaningless by present practice. The state helps the children of public and private schools. It harms the children of parochial schools. It discriminates against them on account of their religion, or more accurately the religion of their parents. There is nothing of neutrality in this; there is nothing of justice in it. Chief Justice Burger, who with Mr. Justice Rehnquist, and Mr. Justice White, dissented in *Meek* v. *Pittenger,* stated the error of the Court clearly and forcefully:

> If the consequence of the Court's holding operated only to penalize *institutions* with a religious affiliation, the result would be grievous

enough; nothing in the Religion Clauses of the First Amendment permits governmental power to discriminate *against* or affirmatively stifle religions or religious activity. But this holding does more: it penalizes *children*—children who have the misfortune to have to cope with the learning process under extraordinary heavy physical and psychological burdens, for the most part congenital. This penalty strikes them not because of any act of theirs but because of their parents' choice of religious exercise. . . .

To hold, as the Court now does, that the Constitution permits the States to give special assistance to some of its children whose handicaps prevent their deriving the benefit normally anticipated from the education required to become a productive member of society and, at the same time, to deny those benefits to other children *only because* they attend a Lutheran, Catholic, or other church-sponsored school does not simply tilt the Constitution against religion; it literally turns the Religion Clauses on their heads.[17]

These are sobering words, indeed, from the Chief Justice of the United States. We have moved from the early period of our history when religion and education were friends, through a period of neutrality when religion and education were tolerant of each other. Now, have we not entered a period where education and religion by means of the process of judicial review become hostile to each other? Is secularism so important and so valuable, so productive of moral fiber and meaning that we can afford to ignore all reference to religion in our elementary and secondary schools? What is the impression that children get of a purely secular system of education? How can they help getting the idea that religion is not important enough to be considered? If we are content with that for ourselves and our children, have we any right to discriminate against parents and children of other persuasions who think that education and religion go hand in hand? Must we make it difficult if not impossible for them, especially as they pay taxes to support public schools, to send their children to parochial schools? In a perilous society like ours do we really wish to eliminate parochial schools, and still say that we believe in freedom of religion? We Protestants ought to take a new look at ourselves and our traditional stance concerning education. I, for one, respectfully dissent from the traditional Protestant view regarding aid to parochial schools. I do not see much chance that tax funds will go to the substantive support of parochial schools. As a matter of simple justice and the free exercise of religion, parochial school students should not be deprived of school lunches, nursing and medical care, psychological testing, aid from trained social workers, or speech therapy. To do so, when public and private school children receive these services in the same city or town, is a violation of the First Amendment's free exercise clause. It is not enough to say that aid to parochial schools might be a good idea. It is required.

7. Abortion and Conscience

In January, 1973, the Supreme Court handed down its landmark decision which invalidated all state restrictions on abortion and gave the United States one of the most liberal abortion programs in the world. The decision has been praised by the proponents of abortion as a document deserving of equal place with the Declaration of Independence. By its opponents the decision has been compared with the Dred Scott decision which sealed the fate of the black man as an inhuman chattel. The implications of *Roe* v. *Wade* and *Doe* v. *Bolton,*[1] decisions made by the Court at the same time, are impossible to calculate and predict. The decisions are, to say the least, sweeping, not only as monumental tracts of judicial review, but also as instruments of legislation, for they call for a complete program of state statutory implementation.

The decisions deserve a careful reading of the entire text, but it is possible to give here only the salient points of the Court's summary of *Roe* v. *Wade*: State criminal abortion laws, like those involved here, that except from criminality only a life-saving procedure on the mother's behalf without regard to the stage of her pregnancy and other interests involved violate the Due Process clause of the Fourteenth Amendment, which protects against state action the right to privacy, including a woman's qualified right to terminate her pregnancy. Though the State cannot override that right, it has legitimate interests in protecting both the pregnant woman's health and the potentiality of human life, each of which interests grows and reaches a "compelling" point at various stages of the woman's approach to term.[2]

(a) For the stage prior to approximately the end of the first trimester, the abortion decision and its effectuation must be left to the medical judgment of the pregnant woman's attending physician.

(b) For the stage subsequent to approximately the end of the first trimester, the State, in promoting its interest in the health of the mother, may, if it chooses, regulate the abortion procedure in ways that are reasonably related to material health.

(c) For the stage subsequent to viability, the State in promoting its interest in the potentiality of human life may, if it chooses, regulate, and even proscribe, abortion except where it is necessary, in appropriate medical judgment, for the preservation of the life or health of the mother.

The State may define the term "physician" . . . to mean only a physician currently licensed by the State, and may proscribe any abortion by a person who is not a physician as so defined.[3]

Doe v. *Bolton* refers to special features of the Georgia statute requiring that abortions be performed in a hospital accredited by the Joint Commission on Accreditation of Hospitals; that the abortion be approved by the hospital staff abortion committee; and that the performing physician's judgment be confirmed by independent examinations of the patient by two other licensed physicians. All three of these restrictions were declared to be invalid.

Another very recent (1976) case, *Planned Parenthood of Central Missouri* v. *Danforth*,[4] is a corollary of *Roe* v. *Wade*, of which there promises to be no end as the special provisions of various state statutes are reviewed. This case further widens the scope of the abortion program which is now in process: The Missouri law had required the consent of the husband before an abortion could be performed. This consent was declared to be an unconstitutional restriction upon the pregnant mother, and the State cannot "delegate to a spouse a veto power which the [S]tate itself is absolutely and totally prohibited from exercising during the first trimester. . . ." The Court also ruled in *Planned Parenthood* that conditioning an abortion on consent of the parents is not required for an unmarried under-18-year-old pregnant minor. The Court cited *Roe*, "the abortion decision and its effectuation must be left to the medical judgment of the pregnant woman's attending physician."[5]

We have reviewed briefly the legal situation with respect to abortion as it now exists in the United States. We are only beginning to know what implications for the future life of the nation and indeed for the world are contained in these recent decisions of the Court. Let us briefly review, for the sake of perspective, what the conditions were which obtained before the Court's decision.

Historically, the law had allowed abortion only as a protection for the mother's health. In recent years, beginning with a reformed statute in Colorado, some liberalization of the law was effected to permit abortion in cases of rape, incest, disease, or malformation of the fetus. Nevertheless, during all the years of history, abortion has been practiced, illegally, brutally, at times fatally, for the mother as well as the fetus. One of the arguments advanced to the courts for abortion reform was the widespread and illegal practice of abortion by nonmedical types, by midwives, by quacks, often with dangerous and unsanitary methods. Contact with these practitioners was often made by clandestine rendezvous in some back alley "clinic," at great cost to the patients involved, with great trauma because of the illegality, and with sometimes fatal results for the mother.

Thus, a woman was trapped. She had no legal choice, no recourse but to carry the child to term or become a criminal, and the criminal act often placed her life in desperate danger.

The burden of this illegal practice lay heavily upon the poor. For the poor and the uninformed particularly often had no help or recourse but to carry the child to term or to abort it by some illegal makeshift and homespun method. The laws of the states were not uniform. A woman could travel to another state for an abortion if such a trip could be afforded. Abortions were constantly performed by licensed physicians, sometimes at great risk to the doctor, sometimes quite routinely in licensed hospitals. But such aid was available usually for the wealthy and the sophisticated only. Abortion laws were liberalized in Europe long before they were changed in America. A trip to London or Sweden for the wealthy was not an uncommon event. As in the case of draft counseling during the recent Vietnam sadness, the benefits of abortion were, and to some extent still are, available to the rich and forbidden to the poor.

Indeed, the 1977 Supreme Court decisions (*Maher* v. *Roe, Beal* v. *Doe,* and *Poelker* v. *Doe*) have the potential of again forbidding abortion, except for therapeutic purposes, to the poor. These decisions state that nothing in the Constitution or the Social Security Act (authorization for Medicaid funding at the federal level) requires states and municipalities to fund elective abortions. Thus, the way seems open for states and cities to deny abortions to the poor, even if attempts at the federal level to do so have so far been unsuccessful.

But what of the present situation since 1973 and the advent of abortion on demand? Here are the statistics of legal abortions for the first three years after the decision:[6]

	1973	1974	1975
Abortions performed	742,460	899,850	988,020
Abortion rate (% of all pregnancies)	16.5	19.5	21.7

More than one-fifth of all pregnancies in 1975, excluding miscarriages, were terminated by legal abortion. There is an overwhelming disparity in the number of abortions performed in urban and rural communities. Although rural areas have relatively few abortions, they also have few hospitals and many of them do not perform abortions. Many rural women have abortions in the big cities.[7]

It is estimated that one-third of all abortions are performed on teenagers. However, it is also estimated that the need for abortion services among teenagers is far greater than the number performed. It is estimated that in 1974, out of 450,000 teenage girls who were in need of abortions, 160,000 were unable to obtain abortion services. In fact, of the 1.3 to 1.8 million women estimated to be in need of legal abortion services in 1974, about 30–50 percent were unable to obtain them. The reason for this is presumed to be lack of facilities, although there is no way of knowing how many women who "needed" abortions did not receive the service because they chose, out of religious or moral scruples or for other reasons, not to do it. In any case, in 1974 only a little more than one-fourth of all non-Catholic general hospitals were identified as having performed abortions. Some hospitals in the public sector performed none.

The number of illegal abortions during the same three years is not known. But, as might be expected, the number of illegal abortion deaths in the United States declined markedly following the Supreme Court's decision of 1973 regarding abortion. Only three illegal abortion deaths were reported in 1975, as opposed to thirty-nine in 1972.[8]

In 1976, it was estimated that over a million abortions would be performed. In 1975, in testimony before Congress, 300,000 abortions are reported to have been paid for under Medicaid, a federally funded, state-operated system of welfare for the elderly and the indigent.

My purpose here is to discuss the very complex question of abortion from the point of view of religious liberty. I have no competence to answer the substantive moral, medical, and legal questions as to whether or not abortion is murder, or when the fetus becomes a human being, or a human person. Does a woman have absolute freedom of her body? Does the fetus have rights? Insofar as I know, nobody has answered these questions satisfactorily. I can say confidently that abortion is killing, and that word is more appropriate, so it seems to me, than the various euphemisms, such as termination of pregnancy, elimination of the fetus, etc. The questions I should like to address myself to are rather: What violations of religious liberty, if any, are involved in abortion? Is the father's religious liberty violated? Is the family's religious liberty protected? How about the doctor who is called upon to implement such a dreadful decision? Is his or her religious liberty put in jeopardy? What about the taxpayer whose money goes to finance abortion under Medicaid?

But the principle question, and the one upon which all the others are based, is the fundamental question of whether or not the Supreme Court's decision violated the religious conscience of a large part of the religious people of the nation. Most proponents of abortion are very sure they know the answer to this. This answer is "no." Pro-abortionists assert that while abortion is a religious question and it does have implications for religious liberty, the religious viewpoints of a particular church concerning abortion prior to *Wade* were being imposed upon the society at large. That is to say, under the previous situation where most abortions were proscribed by law, it was the religious conscience of a particular church (Roman Catholic, mainly) which was inflicted upon the entire populace. Now that the Supreme Court has struck down these religiously offensive laws, the matter, so it is said, has been settled and a victory for religious liberty has been won. This argument is facile and simplistic.

The argument, as it is generally advanced, states that "you cannot legislate morality." The prohibition of abortion, so it is said, was a moral position taken by a particular church which tried to impose its moral views with respect to abortion on the entire society. Does any group have the right to use its muscle to impose its moral views on other citizens who do not share those views? Answering their own questions, the pro-abortionists cite the horrible example of prohibition, that is to say, the Volstead Act. The result of this ill-fated experiment, it is confidently stated by almost everybody, was to "move liquor from the saloons into the speakeasies." I think this classic analogy only clouds the issue. It is undoubtedly true that the Eighteenth Amendment did reflect the moral code of a particular group. But all laws, that is, laws of the proportion and dimension of the prohibition of booze and abortion, reflect the moral code of somebody or some group. The repeal of prohibition in 1934 also represented the moral code of another particular group. The efforts now afoot to lift the legal drinking age from eighteen to nineteen or twenty-one also represents the moral view of a particular group in society. And the Supreme Court decision of 1973, which struck down all state law concerning abortion and began a new era and a new program of liberal abortion laws, of course, represents the moral viewpoint of a sizable segment of the population. It is inevitable that some group of citizens will impose its moral views on a portion of the society which does not share those views. The famous *Brown* v. *Board of Education* decision of 1954[9] was a moral viewpoint which held that black people and particularly black children were equal to any other people and that their rights which had been denied for three centuries should be restored and protected. This viewpoint was justly imposed upon a large number of people who did not share that viewpoint. In a similar manner the Supreme Court decision of 1973 represents a religious or moral position, to be specific, the religious and moral viewpoint of secular humanism, which is probably the predominant religion of America. It is not captious to call secular humanism a religion, for it has been so elevated by the Supreme Court itself in *Torcaso* v. *Watkins*,[10] which is delineated briefly in chapter 4 of this book.

The Court refused in that case to make any distinction between religions which believed in God and those which did not, and specifically named secular humanism as a religion of the latter category. It also asserted a similar doctrine in *United States* v. *Seeger* and *Welsh* v. *United States,* wherein a moral viewpoint, sincerely held, is represented as a sufficient surrogate for traditional religion.[11]

So the upshot of the debate about whether or not in the abortion controversy any particular religion may impose its religious views on society comes down to a nonquestion. For in any case some group's religious values will be imposed on society. In *Roe* the Supreme Court decreed that it should be the religious view of secular humanism which should prevail. Since the religion of secular humanism does not believe in God, nor in any transcendent ingredient in humanity, it finds the killing of fetuses to be a relatively simple operation, having importance only to medicine, to demography, and to the rights of privacy of women.

But in making that judgment, the Court has not settled the religious question. It has simply legislated into law the religious viewpoint of another portion, perhaps a majority, perhaps not, of the populace. In so doing it has offended the religious conscience of those who hold strong convictions that the fetus at some point in the pregnancy, as yet unknown to theology or medicine, is made in the image of God.

The secular humanists would reply that religious rights are not violated by such action, since nobody is being coerced into having an abortion. The traditional religionist would, no doubt, reply that that thesis itself is at least questionable, since the influence of a dominant opinion is always somewhat coercive in a peer-culture situation, and the very ease with which abortions may now be demanded and obtained places immense strain upon the conscience of women, physicians, the spouses and families of pregnant women, and institutions, which hold traditional religious beliefs. Moreover, it places the religious person opposing abortion in the position of having to support by taxation another religious viewpoint and practice which is repugnant. We have said enough to make clear the rather facile and superficial nature of the slogan "No church or religious group has a right to impose its moral code on society." As Paul Ramsey says, ". . . on the question of abortion, each disputant has a religious faith and ethical creed."[12]

The Supreme Court decisions on abortion have put enormous pressure upon the conscience of the physician who performs the abortion. The decision to abort is left entirely to the woman and her doctor. Parents, the husband, the state—all are excluded legally from the decision. Of course, the doctor may refuse to perform the abortion, but then the patient may go elsewhere. So there are immediate pressures on doctors not to refuse. They are professional physicians, and health is their business. The health of the mother is the primary consideration of a physician, even though the term "health of the mother" may be so broadly interpreted as to require the doctor to become something of a sociologist, something of a psychiatrist, something of a clergyman. But good doctors have always performed these wider roles; in fact, they are used to "playing God."

Most physicians are conscientious and do not take the abortion decision lightly. But the very language they use and the spirit of the times in which they live, especially in the medical community, favor abortion. They are pushed to be pro-abortion rather than anti-abortion—unless of course they have religious convictions against it. The semantics of the matter is important. To say, "Abortion is a medical problem, not a moral problem," takes care of the matter for some doctors. Physicians do not refer to "killing the fetus" any more than they refer to "killing the patient" in a terminal situation. They call it "termination of pregnancy," and the rather simple operation is now so common that it is abbreviated to TOP. In the case of a terminal patient they speak of "pulling the tubes," or "the plugs," or "ceasing heroics." Of course, they know that in either case they are ending human life, even though in the cases of abortion they may rationalize that it is only a potential life, while in the case of a terminal patient they are "allowing the patient to die."

Physicians are not on the whole any more or any less religious than other professionals. They have taken an oath to heal, to prolong life. They are, in fact, champions of life, and death is, perhaps, more for them than for the ordinary mortal, an enemy. But some doctors on religious grounds regard abortion as being, at least, in the same species as murder. In such instances, of course, they simply will not perform abortions or have anything to do with the practice. But what of their professional status if they take this hard line? What if they were applying to a prestigious hospital for a residency in obstetrics and gynecology? Would they be accepted? Would they refuse even to counsel a woman as to what her options are with respect to abortion? If they did refuse such counsel, would they be liable for malfeasance suits? And if they do refuse to perform abortions, must they make some kind of referral? Does referral really answer their questions or soothe their scruples to ride piggyback on another doctor's conscience? Is all of this "sound" medical practice? These are the questions which come to mind for the doctor, perhaps any doctor, but certainly for the doctor who believes abortion is wrong.

Out of this dilemma, which I have so briefly sketched, have come "conscience clauses," with which I shall deal later, added to state statutes dealing with abortion in some forty states.

The Supreme Court in *Wade* and *Bolton* deliberately gave to the woman the abortion decision, arguing that since she must bear the child, she shall make the decision as to whether or not she shall abort it. Some state laws had previously required that the husband's consent be obtained. But the *Danforth*[13] decision argued that to require the husband's consent gave him a veto which the state did not itself have and could not therefore bestow on the spouse. However, this argument fails to mention that the husband has a larger interest in the child than the state. In fact, Mr. Justice White points out in dissent, "A father's interest in having a child—perhaps his only child—may be unmatched by any other interest in his life."[14] The father's interest in the child is enhanced if he has religious scruples against the killing of the fetus. It may be assumed that under normal relationships the husband and the prospective mother would consult with each other regarding so grave a decision. Yet in the final analysis there is no protection for the conscience of the husband.

The Court also ruled in *Danforth*[15] that a pregnant unmarried minor need not gain consent of her parents in order to have an abortion, arguing, as in the instance of the father, that since the state had not reserved the right of veto for itself, it could not confer such a right upon the parents. But in making that ruling, it has taken away the parents' right of supervision of minor children, a right which the state does not have inherently but which parents do. It was agreed to in *Wisconsin* v. *Yoder*[16] that parents alone have jurisdiction with regard to the education of children beyond the eighth grade where religious interests with regard to the family tradition are in conflict. In other words, parents are not required to send their children to public schools beyond the elementary level if a religious concern of the family is transgressed. Here in the abortion decision, a matter of supreme, not to say ultimate importance, the family is permitted no jurisdiction at all. When and if the religious convictions of the family are such that abortion is considered murder or something close to it, the interference with the family's religious freedom, it would seem to me, is enormous. Again, the abortion decision is considered a matter of medical importance only. In the case of a pregnant 13- or 14-year-old girl, which is not an uncommon occurrence, it is indeed a medical problem of critical dimension. But abortion may also be a religious and moral question, causing great offense to the family conscience. One may be allowed to hope that in any healthy family relationship the parents would be consulted, and such consultation is not precluded. But it may also be argued that the parents might be the last people the unfortunate girl would go to for counsel, and that she would be more likely to seek the help of her peer group, other minor children. It seems strange to me that the state, which professes so great interest in minor children's education, health, and welfare in other dimensions of life, would not require that a pregnant, unmarried girl seek the best adult advice and help she can get before making the decision to have an abortion. It can only be presumed and hoped that such advice and help would come from her family.

One other concern that has arisen and has even reached the eyes of Congress and the Supreme Court is whether or not Medicaid funds should be used to pay for abortions. Medicaid is a federally funded program usually administered by the several states. The recent Court decisions giving state and local governments the option of funding or not funding abortions leaves the question open. The issue has some comparable dimensions with respect to parochial schools. If it is repugnant for the general public to be taxed to support parochial schools, is it not similarly repugnant for religious people who consider abortion an abomination to support its practice by their taxes? Of course, there are other contiguous arguments which are made with respect to war. The government has never granted any relief from taxation to those who consider war a monstrous violation of the sanctity of human life. The latter question is so huge that the abortion question seems small in comparison. And yet, it is estimated that some three and a half million legal abortions have been performed since 1969, a number far exceeding the lives lost by the United States in all her wars. There were 300,000 abortions, it is estimated, performed under Medicaid in 1975. Should that portion of the citizenry which finds abortion offensive be obliged to pay that huge bill? Some might argue that capital punishment, which is often opposed on religious grounds, is also supported by the taxes of those who find it a violation of religious conscience. But are the two issues of equal weight?

I find the argument for withholding Medicaid funds to pregnant women lacking in force, not because of any comparisons with other practices such as war, but simply on the argument of human need. It would be a cruel and inhuman, not to say punitive, practice to deny abortions to women who are poor when it is not similarly denied to the people who can afford them. I find no solution to the question of religious conscience here. The law simply does not reach all cases of conscience. I suppose it never has. But still the questions should be asked and the comparisons should be made.

In reaction to *Wade* and *Bolton* and the sweeping requirement of the new abortion laws, conscience clauses or conscience laws have been inserted into state statutes in an effort to codify the religious rights of those who are opposed to abortion and to preclude their participation in the abortion process. Physicians and nurses of Roman Catholic or other religious persuasion have sought protection in these clauses out of fear that they might be discriminated against in jobs and medical practice. Denominational hospitals were also afraid that state regulatory agencies might require abortion facilities as a condition for retaining a license. On the other hand, physicians willing to perform abortions felt they might be discriminated against by Catholic or other denominational hospitals.[17]

About forty states have passed such conscience clause laws, varying only slightly from state to state. In general, employment discrimination against persons unwilling to perform abortions is proscribed. Receipt of federal funds under enumerated federal programs does not require recipients, institutional or individual, to perform or assist in the abortion process. Private hospitals may under some conscience clauses also refuse to perform abortions, but presumably these protective clauses do not apply to public hospitals.

Many questions arise out of these clauses: Can an institution have a conscience? Is any hospital in any real and recognizable sense a private institution? Do not all denominational hospitals and all private hospitals serve a public function? Do not all of them receive public funds—Medicaid, Medicare, etc.? Is it not possible to argue that they cannot under the Fourteenth Amendment deny the right of a woman seeking a legal abortion to have it? Are they then to be forced to provide such abortion facilities and operations in violation of religious beliefs protected by the First Amendment? Are the conscience clauses necessary? Are they unconstitutional? It looks as though there will be much work for many lawyers over many years.

Thus, in two or three landmark cases, the Supreme Court of the United States has reversed an historical precedent which had heretofore offered some protection to fetal life. I cannot argue the much-debated point about whether or not the fetus is a human being or at what point the fetus becomes a human being. There is no question that at some point it becomes a human being, and if the pregnancy is allowed to proceed without interruption, a human being will be born, a human being which the Judeo-Christian tradition has proudly, faithfully, and hopefully proclaimed to be made in the image of God. It is a profoundly religious question, then, whether or not anybody may terminate that life, whether human, or only potentially human (which of us is not only "potentially human"?) for any but the most profound reasons. As Ralph Potter says, "The fetus symbolizes you and me and our tenuous hold upon a future here at the mercy of our fellow men." [18]

But it is also a profoundly religious question as to whether or not an unwanted child should come into the world, especially into a world in which the child shall live without love, without sufficient food or shelter, without hope or joy. It is a profoundly religious question as to whether or not a woman shall be obliged to bear a child when she may be already burdened with many other children, often without the support and love of a husband and father. It is a religious question whether or not she shall be able legally to abort a fetus which is to her a burden and a source of despair. The abortion question is not just one question among other questions. It is an ultimate question, and the decision of abortion however it may be anesthetized by crisp and neutral medical terms, such as "termination of pregnancy," or legal phrases, such as "the medical judgment of the pregnant woman's attending physician," is a decision of anguish. It is a religious question whether or not that decision should result in guilt, unrelieved and festering. It is a religious question also whether or not that decision, made perhaps with no other value at stake than that of convenience, should result in indifference and unconcern, and become contagious.

Our society is one which is increasingly preoccupied with rights—rights of minorities, rights of women, etc. The abortion cases and the entire abortion program which is now in process is predicated on the rights of the pregnant woman. It is inevitable that in pressing her rights and thus privatizing ethics, values, and morality, the way is left open for irresponsibility. In abortion, one of the most ultimate values of all is at issue—the dignity and sanctity of human life. And that is not a private concern. Everybody has a stake in the preservation of that value. The business of religion is to uphold values, ultimate values. It is not unconcerned with human rights, but it must always weigh rights against responsibilities.

In the case of abortion, the woman's right to a legal choice has been secured. The rights of the fetus are studiedly ignored. The fetus does have a right to be wanted. That unborn person also has the right to be born for the best motives possible—out of love and not just to hold a marriage together, or to get one started, or to secure an heir, or just because the mother forgot to take the pill. That unborn person to be is, in a sense, already born and become a judge of us and our world. That potential life has a right to be born into a better world than this, a world where human life is not the cheapest commodity on the marketplace, where there is no starvation or famine, war or crime, poverty or despair. But the fetus does have a right to be born into the only world there is, and one which is probably better than the world you and I were born into. If the fetus dies, he or she has a right to die for some greater value than mere convenience. That is the final factor in the cheapening of human life. To those who hold traditional religious views of the sanctity of human life, abortion must always be an offense to conscience. It may not be possible for people of religious conscience to give an unqualified "no" to the abortion question, but neither is it possible to give an unqualified "yes." I repeat myself: Abortion is a decision of anguish.

8. The Exercise of Religious Freedom

"Free from what? I should see it shining in your eyes: Free for what?" —attributed to Nietzche

Protestants have been preoccupied in recent years with the establishment clause of the First Amendment, particularly as it has come under judicial review by the Supreme Court. A large number of Supreme Court decisions have piled up, especially since the First Amendment, again by the process of judicial review, has been applied to the individual states under the Fourteenth Amendment. These decisions, having to do with prayer, Bible reading, released-time in public schools, auxiliary aid to parochial schools (such as busing and textbooks), sabbatarian concerns, tax-exemption for religious organizations, etc., have created a briarpatch of restrictions and limitations upon religion.

Such an immense preoccupation has tended to obscure or overshadow the free-exercise clause, which is the centerpiece of religious freedom, and to give a negative dimension to religious liberty. An inordinate concern about separation of church and state has left religious freedom in a vacuum and has robbed it of substance and content.

The very first principle of religious liberty is not to take such a precious right for granted. The egregious crimes against religious freedom in other parts of the world, the prison farms of the "Gulag Archipelago," the jailing of priests in Brazil, the persecution of Christians in Africa, to mention only a few, are lamented and deplored. But this is not the Soviet Union, or Uganda, or Brazil, and it is assumed that such flagrant violations of religious liberty could not occur in the United States. And perhaps they cannot and will not, but a certain vigilance is always appropriate and necessary.

Certainly there have been violations of human rights in this country during the past twenty years, some of which were infringements of religious liberty. During the fifties and sixties, people engaged in the civil rights movement, which they regarded as a part of their free exercise of religion, were jailed, beaten, and some were killed. Many of these people were ministers, priests, and nuns. Related to the civil rights movement was the opposition to the Vietnam war in which the religious conscience of thousands was offended. Many were jailed and punished for religious viewpoints and, in the case of the Berrigans and others, for religiously symbolic acts. The recent revelations concerning the surveillance and persecution by the FBI of Martin Luther King, Jr., and the mystery which surrounds his death constitute a modern American saga of religious persecution and blackmail. The efforts of the CIA to subvert and use the mission movement abroad and the missionaries as intelligence agents are too numerous to ignore. In an earlier period, during the McCarthy era, Bishop G. Bromley Oxnam of the Methodist Church was subjected to the most extreme limitation of religious freedom by the House Un-American Activities Committee.

In that same era, I remember being called on by two formidable FBI agents in response to letters I had written to J. Edgar Hoover, among others, asking for protection for my friend, Dr. Clarence Jordan, of Americus, Georgia, who was being shot at, bombed, and boycotted in an effort to destroy his religious and interracial community. I soon found that the FBI men were unconcerned about Jordan but were doubtful of my loyalty to the United States and had come to investigate me. This interference in domestic affairs by the FBI and the CIA apparently goes on apace and is a distinct threat to civil rights and religious liberty. We need not be paranoid about our government, but we do need to be watchful. Nobody prizes religious freedom more than those who have lost it.

A second preliminary point is to keep our heads straight as to the relative importance of the two religious clauses of the First Amendment. An undue emphasis on the establishment clause has little yield in religious freedom. Separation of church and state is an auxiliary principle, instrumental but not substantive to the larger doctrine of religious liberty. Protestantism has spent too much time with its rather neurotic fears about some supposed establishment which nobody really wants or seriously predicts. At the same time, we have had the benefit of a *de facto* Protestant establishment which has existed since the beginning of the Republic. It is ungracious, not to say hypocritical, for Protestants to continue in this unproductive vein, especially since we have a decent and respectable tradition of dissent to sustain.

There has never been an absolute separation of church and state in this country, and as long as the same people who make up religion make up the state, and as long as the problems of the state are the problems of religion as well, there cannot be absolute separation.

Many regard Jefferson's metaphor of the wall as being a part of the Constitution, having all the force and sanction of law. This illusion has given rise to the popular notion that "religion and politics don't mix," that "government and religion must have nothing to do with each other," and "that's what separation of church and state means."

This viewpoint, which is an element in pietism, is present in most all religious enterprises. It makes religion the only goal of religion. It seeks to keep religion personal, private, and uninvolved in public affairs and is itself the only wall of separation which has ever existed. Jefferson wanted a pietistic church, and so do modern secularists— that is, a fenced-in, contained, and predictable church which never says a discouraging word to government, education, or any other institution of our culture. Strange paradox it is that pietism which wants so fervently to be religious and wants society to be religious winds up promoting not freedom *of* religion, but freedom *from* religion.

Pietism has been and still is a positive and necessary part of American religion. It is present in any and all denominations, all systems of faith; it is present in all religious people. It is merely a synonym for personal religion. It becomes mischievous when it fosters detachment, denies risk, and hides behind an imaginary wall to protect itself from involvement in the world. At that point it denies the very religious tradition which has given it birth. For pietism has its roots, as do all Western religious movements, in the Judeo-Christian tradition, the tradition of the prophets who thundered and roared against government and society which oppressed the people, the tradition of the New Testament, which clearly states that God loves, not merely the church, not only individuals, but the *world.*

As long as the forces of religion feel guilty of breaking down some imaginary wall every time they involve themselves in politics and government, the church is empty and weak in soul. Suppose that the press saw its freedom, another First Amendment right, in this cabined and confined manner. Instead, the press exercises its freedom in bold, investigative reporting and analysis in an effort to keep the freest nation on earth honest and truthful and thereby continue and buttress its freedom. The role of faith cannot be anything less.

Likewise, the church must exercise its freedom to fulfill its mission in the world. Roger Williams, that great proponent of religious liberty, saw the real danger when he recognized another wall:

> When they have opened a gap in the hedge or wall of separation between the garden of the church and the wilderness of the world, God hath ever broke down the wall itself, removed the candlestick, and made His garden a wilderness, as at this day.[1]

Roger Williams was himself a pietist but of an earlier and healthier Puritan variety. He was concerned to keep the church in the world, ever engaged in public morality and policy, ever a leaven for society's lump. But he was also concerned to keep the world out of the church. The modern church, Protestant and Catholic, tends to reverse the priorities and tries to keep the church out of the world. Preoccupied as it is with private religion, largely oblivious to public policy, it is infiltrated by the world and its values, enthralled with the American way of life, bound by a brooding secularism, held captive in Babylon. No matter what legal sanctions it receives from the state, religion which wanders in that kind of wilderness is not free.

Religion in America is captive to comfort, to status and prestige, to institutional wheeling and dealing. The churches are infiltrated by business and its methods, by government and its bigness, by whatever is popular or faddish in the current scene. Its values are identical with society's values. Its goals are to be big, to be rich, to be powerful, and above all to win. It worships what William James called "the bitch goddess of success."

The religious enterprise resembles nothing so much as a mirror held up to the general culture. Like Narcissus, we look in the pool and what we see we like, and we say, "You are beautiful." Sometimes a signal comes back faintly, "Are you real? Are you just? Are you good? Are you free? Do you love? Whatever happened to the prophets and to Jesus Christ?" And when we read those signals, we want to get out of the culture trap. But how to break out? How do we sing the Lord's song in a strange land?

We must return to the Protestant principle and to an independent position of nonconformity and dissent. "The Protestant principle," says Tillich, "contains the divine and human protest against any absolute claim made for a relative reality, even if this claim is made by a Protestant church. The Protestant principle is the judge of every religious and cultural reality, including the religion and culture which calls itself 'Protestant.'"[2]

Our dissent should be updated by expanding our concepts of what it means to be religious, what it means to be free, and by expanding our action accordingly. We are free to exercise our religion, to pray, to teach, to evangelize, even to be prophetic. But is what we do important, and does it make any difference? Nobody could object to much of anything that comes from our pulpits. If we are prophets, we are for the most part very careful prophets. We are good evangelists, but would it make any difference if everybody were Christian the way we are Christians? The Russians would still be Russians; the Chinese loyalties would be the same; certainly the Americans would still be Americans; and we should all be looking down our missiles at each other. The poor would still be poor; starvation would still be a specter. The rich would still be rich. I suspect a modern Thomas Jefferson would be saying of modern religion what he said of the religious groups in his day: "They are all sound republicans . . . satisfied with their government . . . anxious for reputation . . . friendly."

A first step in the exercise of religious freedom should be for Protestantism and the entire religious enterprise to make serious efforts to achieve unity. The "fifty-seven variety" approach which Protestantism has tolerated and promoted during its history is an anachronism and a contradiction. Religion points toward unity if it points at all toward God. Division is alienation, not only from ourselves and our brothers and sisters in faith but also from the Eternal. We must expand our religious conscience to include one another. Our Christian association, especially between Roman Catholics and Protestants, has in the past had more to do with toleration than liberty. There is excellent opportunity and hope for a permanent change in that historical attitude, a movement from toleration to love. In Protestantism we are more cousins than brothers and sisters even in the main-line denominations. The ecumenical movement, which began with such hope, is now in the doldrums. As to the relationships between "evangelicals" and "liberals," which crosses all denominational lines, the "tie that binds" is tenuous to say the least, having to do at best more with casual acquaintance than community, and at worst reflecting outright animosity and alienation. Such divisiveness is a vast and sullen sin, against God and against freedom. How shall we talk of freedom when we are not free to love one another in the common Judeo-Christian tradition?

A second step is to attempt to rescue religion and religious truth from the great whore of utility to which it has been prostituted. At one time Christians considered their faith a mountain of truth, respected and revered for the sake of truth itself. Science, secularism, and indifference have eroded that mountain. Religious truth is now tolerated only for its utility. It is true if it works, if it serves some "secular purpose," performs some social function, as the Supreme Court has repeatedly stated. We share this embarrassment with all other disciplines which claim to be roads to truth—sociology, psychology, science itself. Religion's problem is different and more serious, however, for it is caught in this pragmatic world with a message which claims to be absolutely true and ultimate. This makes the shame more bitter for having been meretricious like all the rest. See how we do it: "Be religious, tithe and make a lot of money . . . have peace of mind through faith . . . make a big success of your life." In other words, "Seek the kingdom of God, not because it is ultimate, and of absolute importance, but for what you can get out of it."

We were big on missions when the American flag and the American dollar were moving out in imperialism and colonialism. During the two great world wars religion was enlisted to buttress the cause of patriotism. In the fifties religion was enlisted in the cold war: "Be a Christian and fight communism." In the sixties, our slogan was: "Be a Christian and join the revolution." Now the trend is toward quietism, inwardness, mysticism, growing out of the disillusionment of all causes: "Be a Christian and make TA work better." "Be a

Christian and find self-actualization, realization of full potential, an orange grove and a three-car garage."

Thus religion becomes a mere meeter of needs and provider of comforts. It ceases to be an event, as Abraham Heschel says, no longer asking the ultimate questions, let alone answering them. No longer biblical, it has achieved respectability in society and the "*nihil obstat* signed by the social scientists."[3]

Until we take our faith straight, unmixed with various utilitarian goals of our culture, we are not free. Until we begin to write our own agenda, buck the system for the sake of ultimate values, we have nothing much to say about religious freedom, because we have little idea what it is. When we start swimming upstream against the current of the American way, goading and prodding, criticizing and disturbing, we may find we have less freedom than we thought, but we may find also that we like better what we do have and enjoy it more.

The free exercise of religion should be extended to include an updated moral conscience. The Supreme Court in two seminal cases, *United States* v. *Seeger* and *Welsh* v. *United States,* [4] opened wide the legal door to conscience. These two decisions, having to do with the moral objections to war, are a challenge to the religious community to be the goad and gadfly, not only to stretch and widen its own conscience, but also by its witness to expand the conscience of the entire society.

The community of faith is the servant of harmony, beauty, and order in the world. At no other place is that harmony expressed so clearly as in the beauty and integrity of the earth. "The earth is the LORD's and the fulness thereof " (Psalm 24:1). The religious community is called to be the champion of the care and protection of the earth. It is a theological problem that humanity by its exploitation and corruption of nature and its resources is engaged in spoiling its own nest, alienating itself literally from the "ground" of its being. Overpopulation which is at the very core of the ecological problem becomes a prominent part of the burden on religious conscience. Starvation and hunger are the immediate results of overpopulation, causing despair. Despair leads to death and crime and war and loss of a sense of dignity. Human life becomes the cheapest of all commodities. Since the community of faith believes that human beings are created in the image of God, its conscience is thus violated at the very center of its belief and meaning system. Theologically humanity is separated and alienated from the Ground of its Being.

This is the ancient religious problem of sin, expressed in new and desperate dimensions.

The problem of ecology, though vast indeed, presents itself to the religions of the world as a challenge to change their own attitudes and the attitudes of the society about birth control, conservation of energy, elimination of waste, pollution, and gluttony (one of the seven ancient deadly sins).

In the interest of the free exercise of religion the religious conscience should be expanded to include the whole vast subject of human rights. If religion in America, based as it is on the Bible, believes, as it says it does, in the dignity and worth of all human beings because they are made in the image of God, then it is a part of the conscience of that faith to believe in the rights of life, political liberty, some measure of personal safety and privacy, economic security, free speech, and a free press as the established fundamental rights of human beings.

These rights are clearly stated in the Universal Declaration of Human Rights as set forth by the United Nations General Assembly in 1948. One of these rights is, of course, religious liberty. But in a real sense all rights are religious rights. And it may be argued that all rights stem from the one basic fundamental right of religious freedom. In any case the religious community is required to continue strenuously a ceaseless advocacy for religious freedom throughout the world. The church, or organized religion of all kinds and all creeds, should be united in this effort. The church can make such advocacy and criticize and condemn countries who do not grant religious freedom (the list of such countries is growing) without risk of the charge of interference in domestic affairs of a foreign power. Where governments are embarrassed at such interference, the church and the religious enterprise should be inventing new and creative methods to accomplish such interference.

The entire range of the rights of men and women is included in the religious conscience. A large order indeed it is, but which of the fundamental rights could be rejected or dropped out? It is fair to say, if some choice must be made, that the religious community and conscience should be sensitive to and engaged in protecting the precise rights which are being violated, but especially the rights of the poor and helpless, the victims of society. Rights, however, are neither absolute nor without distinction and priority. The right to strike is less important than free speech. The right to carry guns is of a lower level than the right to safety on the streets. All rights are accompanied by responsibilities and obligations. The religious conscience will recognize that many distinctions and choices must be made, not the least of which is that a person may have all the rights in the book and still be empty and unfree.

In the free exercise of religion a certain conflict or creative tension is inevitable. Like a fine blade, freedom must have a hard steel to work against. One of the natural opponents of religion is the state. In this country the tension and conflict have resulted not so much in hostility as in creativity. The realm of faith proceeds and prospers only by free persuasion. The state possesses power to coerce, and when push comes to shove, it will use it. By and large, in America, the church and the state have been friends, but the friendship is unequal. There are points at which religion must oppose the state to save its own soul. There is always a point where the state will use the church and religion for its own purposes and security even though it claims to be a "nation under God." History is replete with examples. Both sides in the Civil War used the church to buttress its war aims: religion was used to promote the Spanish-American War and both world wars. Both the Kaiser and Hitler used the German church, both Protestant and Catholic, to incite patriotic fervor for the fatherland; Stalin enlisted the church for the support of Holy Russia.

The church must resist these attempts at subversion. An example of such resistance occurred during the Vietnam War when Clergy and Laymen Concerned about Vietnam and Students for a Democratic Society, together with many ministers and lay people from the churches, mounted a movement of massive disobedience to oppose the war effort. They challenged the draft by means of draft counseling centers and were powerfully influential in forcing the downfall of a sitting president, certainly shortening the war, if not ending it. While not all this protest was religious, either specific or inchoate, still all such civil disobedience appealed to a "higher law," which makes no sense except as a religious reference. Whatever the authority invoked, the fact is now generally conceded that the protesters were right, and their silencers and detractors were wrong. A model exists here for the free exercise of religion.

Another model of the exercise of religious freedom was the attempt to gain amnesty for draft dodgers and deserters who for reasons of conscience, either religious or moral, fled the country, mostly to Canada. While this attempt was abortive, since pardon which is considerably less than amnesty was all that was achieved, the attempt is still an example of how religion makes its witness to gain freedom for itself and others.

The general society is the more subtle and more powerful opponent of religion. The churches and religious enterprises which simply "go along" with the society and never mount any opposition to it are simply not "exercising" either their religion or their freedom. Perhaps the best entry for religion into the consciousness of the society is by means of education. Since religion has largely been removed from public schools, most churches have had to be satisfied with their own worship and church-based education programs. There are one or two doors still open into the public sector. The Bible may still be taught as literature, and the religious enterprise could train teachers to give elementary and secondary students a view of the Bible which is reverent and critical. A second possible doorway into the public schools might be to revive the old released-time program, which may be conducted legally off school property. All such a program needs is the will to do it.

Parochial schools are an important part of American society and religion. Some people complain about their "quality" of education. But perhaps many more people complain about the "quality," or lack thereof, in public education. The fact is, the religious enterprise needs parochial schools. To let them die is simply to put further loads upon public schools in the number of pupils and increased taxation. Some relief to parochial schools for auxiliary purposes has been available, as I have stated elsewhere in this book. These services are neutral insofar as religion is concerned, but they do aid parochial school children. Since this aid is available to all other children in private and public schools by federal law, to deny it to parochial school children is to penalize them for their religion and is a gross violation of the First Amendment. All this aid is now threatened, but large Protestant support for it would no doubt restore it. Such action would take courage, and it would be an exercise of religious freedom.

At the college level, of course, the educational program is no less secular than at the elementary and secondary levels. At all levels by ignoring religion we are saying to modern young people, "Religion is not important enough to be included in the curriculum." This subtle put-down is not only destructive of religion but also it is inadequate education. In college we should be making the bold statement: "You cannot have anything close to "quality" education without knowing about religion, because it is the foundation of your culture. You cannot know your heritage; you cannot know who you are apart from a knowledge of religion." A door is open at the college level to found and continue religious departments in state colleges and universities. Our denominational schools, by and large, are good and important, but inadequate for the magnitude of the task. Public education at the college level is an area which calls for imaginative and learned exercise of religious freedom.

Protestants have a long tradition of freedom and dissent, but with the necessity and the incentive gone, we have more the history of it than the present reality. How can we possess our possessions? How can we recover what we already have? How do we "exercise" the muscles we have had little occasion to use in recent years? How do we stand fast in liberty? More importantly, how do we stop standing fast and move on?

One thing is sure; freedom cannot be legislated either by legislators or judges. The Thirteenth, Fourteenth, and Fifteenth Amendments to the Constitution were designed, presumably, to guarantee the civil rights of freedmen. One hundred years later black people still fight for and sometimes get justice under the law (to say nothing of the American Indians). That should forever convince us of the inadequacy of legislation and the entire legal system to assure justice and freedom. Not that it would be easier to get freedom without the law. Mere anarchy and irresponsibility are as severe tyrants as legalism. For as Justice Learned Hand once said: "Liberty lies in the hearts of men and women. . . ."[5] We must depend on a passion rather than a statute to secure religious and civil liberty for ourselves and for others of religious persuasions and cultural differences which may be quite strange, not to say odious, to us.

In the pursuit of this passion for freedom, we must stick to our last. Religious freedom is a theological goal. We must be true to the gospel, for its truth and discipline make men free. That does not mean withdrawal to a stained-glass, monkish view of our role. We are citizens of the world. Our message is a religious message, but as the Old Testament prophets instruct us, it brings all else into its purview. We are not economists, but we must call the economists into judgment on the basis of conscience. We are not politicians, but we must hold the politicians' feet to the fire of justice and morality. We are not psychologists or sociologists, but we hold both those disciplines to account in terms of a transcendent vision. Above all, we must reserve the sharpest and most delicate calipers to measure ourselves. Remembering our past sins against liberty, we must constantly heed the reminder of Cromwell: "I beseech you, in the bowels of Christ, think it possible you may be mistaken."[6]

Notes

Chapter 2

[1] Joseph Story, *Commentary on the Constitution of the United States* (Boston: Little, Brown & Company, 1873), pp. 605, 606.

[2] Thomas Jefferson, *Life and Selected Writings* (New York: Modern Library Books, imprint of Random House, Inc., 1944), p. 332.

[3] *McCollum* v. *Board of Education,* 333 US 247 (1948).

[4] *Ibid.*

[5] Dr. Thomas Cooper, an English scientist who lived in America, a friend of Joseph Priestley, was much admired and sought after by Jefferson. He got Cooper an appointment at the University of Virginia, but Cooper never assumed it because of an uproar in the state over his religious and political views. He went instead to Columbia College, South Carolina, where he taught mineralogy, law, and chemistry.

—Dictionary of American Biography

[6] Thomas Jefferson, *op. cit.,* p. 697.

[7] *McCollum* v. *Board of Education, op. cit.*

[8] The doctrine that the limitations of the First Amendment are applicable through the Fourteenth to the states was first advanced by the Supreme Court in *Cantwell* v. *Connecticut* and enunciated again with great force in *Everson* v. *Board of Education.*

Chapter 3

[1] John Collier, *The Indians of the Americas* (New York: W. W. Norton and Co., 1947), p. 195. Captain John Mason, a New Englander, had left Massachusetts to serve the Dutch in New York as a mercenary.

[2] Gustavus Myers, *History of Bigotry in the United States,* rev. ed. (New York: Capricorn Books, subsidiary of G. P. Putnam's Sons, 1960).

[3] Conrad Cherry, ed., *God's New Israel* (Englewood Cliffs, N.J.: Prentice-Hall, Inc., 1971), pp. 88-89.

[4] *Newsweek,* February 19, 1973.

[5] *Ibid.*

[6] Robert N. Bellah, *The Broken Covenant* (New York: The Seabury Press, Inc., 1975), p. 151.

Chapter 4

[1] *Presbyterian Church* v. *Hull Church,* 393 US 440 (1969).

[2] See *Church of the Holy Trinity* v. *United States,* 143 US 226 (1892). Many similar references are found in other Supreme Court decisions. Also in this decision, "the Christian religion is a part of the common law of Pennsylvania." See also *United States* v. *Macintosh,* 283 US 605 (1931).

[3] *United States* v. *Seeger,* 380 US 163 (1965) and *Welsh* v. *United States,* 398 US 333 (1970).

[4] *Brown* v. *Board of Education,* 347 US 483 (1954).

[5] *Roe* v. *Wade,* 410 US 113 (1973) and *Doe* v. *Bolton,* 410 US 179 (1973).

[6] *Cantwell* v. *Connecticut,* 310 US 296 (1940).

[7] *Minersville School District* v. *Gobitis,* 310 US 586.

[8] Universal Military Training and Service Act, *U. S. Code Annotated,* App., Section 456 (j).

[9] *United States* v. *Seeger,* 380 US 163 (1965), p. 176.

[10] *Welsh* v. *United States,* 398 US 333 (1970), p. 337.

[11] *Walz* v. *Tax Commission of the City of New York,* 397 US 664 (1970), p. 678, quoted from *Jackman* v. *Rosenbaum Co.,* 260 US 22 (1922), p. 31.

[12] *Pierce* v. *Society of Sisters of Holy Names,* 69 L Ed. 1071 US (1925), p. 1078.

[13] *Everson* v. *Board of Education,* 330 US 1 (1947), pp. 15-16.

[14] *Ibid.,* p. 16.

[15] *Ibid.,* p. 18.

[16] *Ibid.,* p. 19.

[17] *Engel* v. *Vitale,* 370 US 421 (1962), p. 422.

[18] *Ibid.,* pp. 424, 425.

[19] *Abington School District* v. *Schempp,* 374 US 203 (1963), p. 229.

[20] *Ibid.,* p. 225.

[21] *Board of Education* v. *Allen,* 228 NE 2d 791, NY (1967).

[22] *Meek* v. *Pittenger,* 43 LW 4596, 421 US 349 (1975), p. 4597.

[23] *McCollum* v. *Board of Education,* 333 US 204 (1948), p. 227.

[24] *Ibid.,* pp. 246, 247.

[25] *Zorach* v. *Clauson,* 343 US 308 (1952), pp. 312, 313.

[26] *Ibid.,* p. 317.

[27] *Ibid.,* p. 325.

[28] *Lemon* v. *Kurtzman,* 403 US 602 (1971).

Chapter 5

[1] *Everson* v. *Board of Education,* 330 US 1 (1947).

[2] *New York Trust Co.* v. *Eisner,* 256 US 345 (1921), p. 349.

[3] *Walz* v. *Tax Commission of the City of New York,* 397 US 664 (1970).

[4] Paul G. Kauper, "Government and Religion, The Search for Absolutes," Russel Lectures, University of Michigan, 1971, *Law Quadrangle Notes,* vol. 15, no. 3 (Spring, 1971), p. 22. I have leaned heavily upon Professor Kauper's work in this chapter. In fact, almost everything I have attempted to say here I learned from him.

[5] Quoted in *Abington School District* v. *Schempp,* 374 US 205 (1963), p. 215.

[6] *Ibid.,* p. 226.

[7] *Walz* v. *Tax Commission of the City of New York*, 397 US 664 (1970).

[8] *Jackman* v. *Rosenbaum Co.*, 260 US 22 (1922), p. 31.

[9] *Lemon* v. *Kurtzman; Earley* v. *DiCenso*, 403 US 602 (1971).

[10] *Board of Education* v. *Allen*, 392 US 236 (1968).

[11] *Meek* v. *Pittenger*, 43 LW 4596, 421 US 349 (1975).

[12] *Zorach* v. *Clauson*, 343 US 308 (1952).

[13] *McCollum* v. *Board of Education*, 333 US 204 (1948).

[14] *Federal Register*, vol. 41, no. 29 (Feb. 11, 1976), Treasury Department, IRS (26 CFR Part 1), 1. 6033-2.

Chapter 6

[1] Edd Doerr, "The Enduring Controversy: Parochiaid and the Law," *Valparaiso University Law Review*, vol. 9 (1975), p. 522.

[2] *Everson* v. *Board of Education*, 330 US 1 (1947).

[3] James Bryant Conant, *Education and Liberty* (Cambridge: Harvard University Press, 1953), p. 81.

[4] Will Herberg, "Religion, Democracy and Public Education," in *Religion in America*, ed. John Cogley (New York: Meridian Books, 1958), p. 127.

[5] *Pierce* v. *Society of Sisters*, 268 US 510 (1925).

[6] *Everson* v. *Board of Education*, 330 US 1 (1947).

[7] *McCollum* v. *Board of Education*, 333 US 203 (1948).

[8] *Zorach* v. *Clauson*, 343 US 306 (1952).

[9] *Board of Education* v. *Allen*, 392 US 306 (1968).

[10] *Lemon* v. *Kurtzman*, 403 US 602 (1971).

[11] *Earley* v. *DiCenso*, 39 LW 4844 (1971), p. 4845.

[12] *Meek* v. *Pittenger*, 43 LW 4596, 421 US 349 (1975).

[13] 74 Civ. 2648, *Pearl* v. *Arthur Levitt*.

[14] *New York Times*, July 14, 1976, letter to the Editor, "Of Church, State and Cooperation" by Msgr. Harry J. Bryne. © 1976 by The New York Times Company. Reprinted by permission of The New York Times Company and Msgr. Bryne.

[15] *Abington School District* v. *Schempp*, 374 US 203 (1963).

[16] *Engel* v. *Vitale*, 370 US 421 (1962).

[17] *Meek* v. *Pittenger*, 43 LW 4596 at 4603, 421 US 349 (1975).

Chapter 7

[1] *Roe* v. *Wade*, 410 US 113 (1973); *Doe* v. *Bolton*, 410 US 179 (1973).

[2] *Roe* v. *Wade*, op. cit., pp. 147-164.

[3] *Ibid.*, pp. 164-165.

[4] *Planned Parenthood of Central Missouri* v. *Danforth*, 44 LW 5197 (July, 1976).

[5] *Roe* v. *Wade*, op. cit., p. 164.

[6] Weinstock, Tietze, et al, "Abortion Need and Services in the United States " (1974–75), Family Planning, *Perspectives*, vol. 8, no. 2 (March–April, 1976).

[7] This paragraph and the following are taken from *ibid.*

[8] Willard Coles, Jr., and Roger W. Rochot, "Illegal Abortions in the US, 1972-74," *Perspectives, op. cit.*

[9] *Brown* v. *Board of Education*, 347 US 483 (1954).

[10] *Torcaso* v. *Watkins*, 367 US 488 (1961).

[11] *Welsh* v. *United States*, 398 US 333 (1970): *United States* v. *Seeger*, 380 US 163 (1965).

[12] Paul Ramsey, "Points on Deciding About Abortion," chapter in *The Morality of Abortion, Legal and Historical Perspectives*, ed. John T. Noonan, Jr. (Cambridge: Harvard University Press, 1970), p. 62.

[13] *Planned Parenthood of Central Missouri* v. *Danforth,* p. 5202.

[14] *Ibid.,* p. 5209.

[15] *Ibid.,* p. 5203.

[16] *Wisconsin* v. *Yoder,* 406 US 205 (1972).

[17] The subject of conscience laws is covered in great detail in Marc D. Stern, "Abortion Conscience Clauses," *Columbia Journal of Law and Social Problems,* Summer, 1975, p. 571. Also in G. Michael White, "Michigan Abortion Refusal Act," *University of Michigan Journal of Legal Reform,* vol. 8 (Spring, 1975), p. 659.

[18] Ralph B. Potter, Jr., "The Abortion Debate," in *The Religious Situation,* ed. Donald R. Cutler (Boston: Beacon Press, 1968), p. 157.

Chapter 8

[1] Quoted by Mark DeWolfe Howe in *The Garden and the Wilderness* (Chicago: University of Chicago, 1965), p. 1.

[2] Paul Tillich, *The Protestant Era* (Chicago: University of Chicago, 1957), p. 163.

[3] Abraham J. Heschel, "The Religious Message," from *Religion in America,* ed. John Cogley (New York: Meridian Books, 1958).

[4] *United States* v. *Seeger,* 380 US 163 (1965); *Welsh* v. *United States,* 398 US 333 (1970).

[5] Irving Dilliard, ed., *The Spirit of Liberty,* 3rd rev. ed. (New York: Vintage Books, Inc., 1959), p. 190.

[6] "Letter to the General Assembly of the Church of Scotland, 3 Aug. 1650," in the *Oxford Dictionary of Quotations.*

Bibliography

American Friends Service Committee, *Who Shall Live? Man's Control Over Birth and Death.* New York: Hill & Wang, 1970.

Augenstein, Leroy, *Come, Let Us Play God.* New York: Harper & Row, Publishers, 1969.

Bellah, Robert, *The Broken Covenant: American Civil Religion in Time of Trial.* New York: The Seabury Press, Inc., 1975.

Brody, Baruch, *Abortion and the Sanctity of Human Life: A Philosophical View.* Cambridge, Mass: MIT Press, 1975.

Callahan, Daniel, *Abortion: Law, Choice, and Morality.* New York: Macmillan, Inc., 1970.

Cherry, Conrad, ed., *God's New Israel, Religious Interpretations of American Destiny.* Englewood Cliffs, N.J.: Prentice-Hall, Inc., 1971.

Cogley, John, ed., *Religion in America.* Cleveland: World Publishing Co., 1958.

Cohen, Carl, *Civil Disobedience, Conscience, Tactics and the Law.* New York: Columbia University Press, 1971.

Collier, John, *Indians of the Americas*. New York: Mentor Books, imprint of New American Library, Inc., 1952.

Commager, Henry S., *Documents of American History*. New York: Appleton-Century-Crofts, 1969.

Cutler, Donald R., ed., *The World Year Book of Religion, The Religious Situation: 1968,* see "The Abortion Debate," by Ralph B. Potter, Jr. Boston: Beacon Press, 1968.

Eliot, Thomas S., *The Family Reunion*. New York: Harcourt Brace Jovanovich, Inc., 1964.

Handy, Robert T., *A Christian America: Protestant Hopes and Historical Realities*. New York: Oxford University Press, 1971.

Herberg, Will, *Protestant, Catholic, Jew: An Essay in American Religious Sociology*. Garden City, N.Y.: Anchor Books, imprint of Doubleday & Co., Inc., 1955.

Howe, Mark DeWolfe, *The Garden and the Wilderness*. Chicago: University of Chicago Press, 1965.

Hudson, Winthrop S., *American Protestantism*. Chicago: University of Chicago Press, 1961.

Kauper, Paul G., *Civil Liberties and the Constitution*. Ann Arbor: University of Michigan Press, 1962.

_____, *Religion and the Constitution*. Baton Rouge: Louisiana State University Press, 1964.

Koch, Adrienne; and Peden, William, eds., *The Life and Selected Writings of Thomas Jefferson*. New York: The Modern Library, 1944.

Mayer, Milton, *On Liberty: Man v. the State*. Santa Barbara: Center for the Study of Democratic Institutions, 1969.

Morgan, Richard E., *The Politics of Religious Conflict*. New York: Pegasus (Publishing), 1968.

_____, *The Supreme Court and Religion*. New York: The Free Press, 1972.

Muller, Herbert J., *Issues of Freedom, World Perspectives,* vol 23. New York: Harper & Row, Publishers, 1960.

Myers, Gustavus, *History of Bigotry in the United States.* New York: Capricorn Books, subsidiary of G. P. Putnam's Sons, 1960.

Niebuhr, Reinhold, *The Irony of American History.* New York: Charles Scribner's Sons, 1952.

Noonan, John T., Jr., ed., *The Morality of Abortion.* Cambridge, Mass.: Harvard University Press, 1970.

Oaks, Dallin H., ed., *The Wall Between Church and State.* Chicago: University of Chicago Press, 1963.

Oxnam, G. Bromley, *I Protest.* New York: Harper & Row, Publishers, 1954.

Richey, Russell E.; and Jones, Donald G., eds., *American Civil Religion.* New York: Harper & Row, Publishers, 1974.

Tillich, Paul, *The Protestant Era.* Chicago: University of Chicago Press, 1957.

Waltz, Kenneth N., *Man, the State, and War.* New York: Columbia University Press, 1959.

Legal Journals

Kauper, Paul G., "The Walz Decision: More on the Religion Clauses of the First Amendment," *Michigan Law Review,* vol. 69, no. 2 (December, 1970).

Stern, Marc D., "Abortion Conscience Clauses," *Columbia Journal of Law and Social Problems,* Summer, 1975.

Valparaiso University Law Review, vol. 9, no. 3 (Spring, 1975).

White, Michael, "Michigan Abortion Refusal Act," *University of Michigan Journal of Legal Reform,* vol. 8 (Spring, 1975).

Index